Dr. Fred Phillips is a serious researcher and aikidoka who has incorporated his lifelong aikido training philosophy into this book. This book is not a technical treatise, but practicing aikidoka should keep its well-organized ideas in mind at all times. I recommend reading it.

Yoon, Dae Hyun, Shihan
Chairman of the Korean Aikido Federation

Great insights! Well written and entertaining.

Paul Barrett, 4th Dan
Dojo-cho, Duke City Dojo, Albuquerque

Thumbs up! Wonderful writing and an amazing Aikido contribution, "The 3-inch-wide black belt arms only the waist. The real black belt is the spiritual practice and the whole body."

Jie Han, 4th Dan
Kobayashi Aikido China and New Zealand

Fred Phillips is the essence of an accomplished Aikido instructor — he delves deep intellectually like the college professor he is, but he also has the heart and soul of a warrior. *Learning and Teaching Aikido* reflects the author's many years of aikido teaching and practice, his continual search for deeper meaning, and his gentle humor. Despite style differences, there are deep principles that are of interest to all of us who train. I believe this book is a worthwhile addition to every martial artist's library.

James Pounds
7th Dan — Goju-Ryu Karatedo Seiwakai
President, Seiwakai USA

Learning and Teaching Aikido is written with mature and sage advice for the modern warrior in modern times. Using humor and irony, Fred Phillips reflects on the words of his teachers. He shares his stories as a reflection, like a Zen meditation, that has informed both his aikido practice and his connection to the world. His stories describe a way of being, with open-mindedness and empathy. He instructs the reader to show up, be present, listen, bring intention, and practice regularly and patiently.

Dan Penrod, 5th Dan
Dojo-cho, Budo Dojo, Beaverton, OR

Learning and Teaching
Aikido

Fred Phillips

University of New Mexico, USA

World Scientific

NEW JERSEY · LONDON · SINGAPORE · BEIJING · SHANGHAI · HONG KONG · TAIPEI · CHENNAI · TOKYO

Published by

World Scientific Publishing Co. Pte. Ltd.
5 Toh Tuck Link, Singapore 596224
USA office: 27 Warren Street, Suite 401-402, Hackensack, NJ 07601
UK office: 57 Shelton Street, Covent Garden, London WC2H 9HE

Library of Congress Cataloging-in-Publication Data
Names: Phillips, Fred, 1952– author.
Title: Learning and teaching aikido / Fred Phillips.
Description: Hackensack, New Jersey : World Scientific, [2021]
Identifiers: LCCN 2021020081 | ISBN 9789811230578 (hardcover) |
    ISBN 9789811230585 (ebook for institutions) | ISBN 9789811230592 (ebook for individuals)
Subjects: LCSH: Aikido. | Aikido--Training.
Classification: LCC GV1114.35 .P55 2021 | DDC 796.815/4--dc23
LC record available at https://lccn.loc.gov/2021020081

British Library Cataloguing-in-Publication Data
A catalogue record for this book is available from the British Library.

For any available supplementary material, please visit
https://www.worldscientific.com/worldscibooks/10.1142/12108#t=suppl

Cartoons by David Wykes
Photo credits outdoors: Patrick Hudson
Photo credits indoors: Paul Barrett
Ukes in photos: Kenneth Hunter and Hyonsook Phillips

Dedicated to aikido students everywhere,
for whom this book is my legacy.

Contents

◄○►

Preface: Why This Book?

◂◦▸

I hope and expect that you have a very fine aikido teacher — or that you are one. Yet I've bet the hours of writing this book against the probability that, with nearly 50 years of aikido experience, I can offer useful thoughts that your teacher has not yet conveyed to you. (Or that you, as teacher, have not yet bestowed on your students.)

Lots of books and videos teach you aikido techniques. Not this book. This book is something different. It is about principles and perspectives on learning and teaching aikido.

There are now more than two million aikido practitioners worldwide. Yet most of the two million practice far from the source (the Aikikai Honbu, or whichever Japanese mother ship their dojo reveres) and under teachers who are now descended three or four generations from the founder and his direct students. This is not something to complain about; it is a necessary result of our art's growth and continuity.

Yet it must be managed. Most aikido federations manage it by standardizing curriculum more tightly. You can appreciate the tension this creates: Students want and need to master a great variety of movements, and to experience a big variety of attack-defense situations. Yet federation requirements imply that almost all class time must be devoted to techniques that appear on the promotion sheet. In the extreme, this means "teaching to the test," and we've seen how badly that works, for example in elementary and high school education in America.

That tension, too, is a lucky thing. If worldwide aikido were not managed in this way, it would deteriorate into ever-splintering factions and ultimately to dojos of highly questionable qualification. (We may argue about whether this has already happened, but we can agree that we don't want it to get worse.)

So this book will assume that your dojo practices basic technique and beyond, under very good teachers; that those techniques fill up class time for two or three practice days per week; and that reading and thinking about *why* you practice what you practice is extracurricular activity. Likewise for ideas and principles that affect *how* you approach and comprehend aikido technique.

This book presents thoughts on "why and how," in bite-sized chapters. Later in the book, longer chapters explore aikido topics of broader scope.

My Japanese senseis in the 1970s wanted Americans of my generation to be pioneers of aikido in the USA and beyond.[1] They sent us out to open dojos and to teach, though we had only the kind of "questionable qualifications" I mentioned above. Some of my contemporaries dropped out of aikido, while others tried hard to live up to our teachers' expectations.

(I tell you this so you'll understand that I want, through this book, to spare you much of the challenge that my peers and I faced. While we're resting comfortably here between parentheses, I'll mention that when I was a just-hatched shodan, my new employer was going to send me to live in Connecticut. I asked my sensei Rod Kobayashi, where should I practice? He replied that I should start my own dojo, building technique from the underlying principles he and Koichi Tohei Sensei had taught me. My unspoken response

---

[1] Second-generation pioneers, to be sure. Western pioneers of the first generation — personages such as Frank Duran, Christian Tissier, Robert Nadeau, and some still more senior — are well known, though few in number.

was, "Yeah, right." When my company changed its mind and instead sent me to Chicago, Rod Sensei said, "Oh, in that case, train under Mr. Toyoda." My feeling of relief was palpable. Yet, in anticipation of having to be a dojo-cho before I felt ready, I had begun to think about how I approach technique, and how I would decide what and how to teach. I believe that mode of thinking served me well, and it informs the chapters of this book. And just to show there's no escaping fate, a few years later Toyoda Sensei insisted that I start a dojo.)

I'm proud that our pioneering mission succeeded. There were several thousand aikido practitioners in the 1970s, and more than two million now. Where we had to travel considerable distances to hone our skills at seminars, you now (probably) have convenient geographic access to high-ranking instructors.

You will be the nth generation of leaders spreading the Art of Peace throughout the world.

You will balance physical aikido practice with mental practice. The next pages are grist for mental practice. It is an adjunct to physical practice, but no substitute for it! The two feed each other.

Enjoy, and *ganbatte kudasai!*

Introduction: May We Disagree?

—◄◦►—

I sure hope so. Some of what you'll see here are things my teachers said, that resonated with me and helped shape my teaching. Other things I've concluded on my own, after practicing and teaching for nearly 50 years.

Yet your experience and your teachers' might give you different perspectives. If you have advanced in black belt ranks and made aikido your own, different views than mine may touch you most deeply.

And as you advance, ideas you once thought profound may now strike you as banal, and teachings you once dismissed as superficial and obvious now take on deep meaning.

That's okay! Even O-Sensei's closest disciples taught with different emphases and took divergent paths.

Argue with me on Facebook if you wish. Tell me how this book gave you and your peers grist for discussion.

Here's what to expect as you read these chapters.

The first section, "Especially for Students," starts with Q&A for raw beginners, but is mostly written for those of you who have trained in aikido for at least several months, and have begun to look beyond the mechanics of basic technique. You have begun to wonder why we do what we do, and what principles underlie the techniques. You are looking for an "edge" to accelerate your learning, deepen your understanding, and keep you motivated.

Some of these chapters are about your role as nage, some about how to be a better uke, some about self-defense, and some about

your relation to your dojo and to your teacher. They are arranged more or less in the order you will need them as your aikido practice progresses.

Students should read the book's second section too, though the section is especially for teachers. Some mini-chapters here are teaching tips. Others dive into matters that teachers can find hard to articulate to students. Likewise, teachers may find value in the "especially for students" chapters.

A third section contains longer chapters. These deal with philosophical and strategic questions that are pertinent to aikido practice.

Thumb back to the "Glossary" section whenever you read an unfamiliar Japanese word.

After the Glossary, you'll find more information About the Author. However, in brief: Though I was a member of Ki Society for only about six years in the 1970s, I did train directly with Koichi Tohei Sensei, and his teachings inform important parts of what you'll read here. My next teacher (after Rod Kobayashi) was Fumio Toyoda Shihan, who had been Tohei's direct student prior to the parting of their ways. Toyoda persevered as head of the independent Aikido Association of America for some decades and ultimately affiliated AAA with World Aikikai Honbu. Yet his instruction continued to build on the foundation Tohei had laid, supplemented by Toyoda's Zen practice. In the twenty years since we lost Toyoda Sensei, I've trained with the Korea and the Taiwan Aikido Federations, both Aikikai-affiliated, and for shorter times with Iwama and Tendo-Ryu schools. My aikido teaching now emphasizes balance (uke's and nage's), posture and positioning, growing our awareness, and learning about our bodies so that we increase our power by not working against ourselves.

The paragraph above is just for your information. Don't worry about it. No matter what your style or school, you can apply this book's advice to your practice, in your dojo, without fear of "being different."

My thanks go out to this book's beta readers and endorsers, to David Wykes for his brilliant cartoons, and to all aikido friends who have helped shape my aikido experience and thus this book.

ESPECIALLY FOR STUDENTS

1

Q&A: Aikido and Martial Art Practice

-◄◦►-

These questions were asked by readers of my earlier book,[2] by my aikido students in class, and by martial artists who replied to my Facebook invitations for topics to address in this book.

Q. I am looking to get back into the martial arts. I have taken tae kwon do for 2 years and attained a green belt. I would like advice on what to pursue for a ground defense/grappling technique. Also will this fit in with my TKD experience? Thank you for your time.

A. *Aikido does not emphasize ground technique — for good reason, I think, but the choice is yours. Try jujitsu for strong groundwork. You will probably find that neither aikido nor jujitsu will build on your TKD experience. They are both very different.*

Q. It seems that Aikido is geared for people who do NOT desire to feel the "joy" of putting people in hospitals (or morgues), but are realistic enough to know that this is not an ideal world. Is this so?

A. *Exactly.*

Q. I have read that Aikido tends to be highly stylized. For example, "if someone grabs you here and here, you do this and this." Any comment?

---

[2] The Conscious Manager: Zen for Decision Makers. ISBN: 978-1581510799

A. *It has to be that way for beginners, because the movements are complex and a certain amount of rote learning is unavoidable. At more advanced levels, aikido is more free-form.*

Q. I have read that many Aikido moves are devastating. If Aikido is indeed partially based on jiu jitsu, I can understand that. I don't want to fight anyone, however, if I must, then I want to do what has to be done. Does Aikido indeed offer truly effective defensive techniques?

A. *Aikido allows escalation of force to the extent necessary. But almost all moves can treat the attacker very gently. After all, many physical conflicts today are of the "my-brother-in-law-was-just-drunk-he-didn't-really-want-to-hurt-me-and-I-didn't-want-to-hurt-him" variety.*

Q. I am old (52), out of condition, and uncoordinated. Would I still be welcome as a student?

A. *We have a lot of members who are at least one of those things, if not all three ;-) You're very welcome to train with us, and if you hang in there you'll enjoy the results. BTW, I envy your youth.*

Q. Should Aikido be fun? I've trained with excellent aikidoists who are VERY serious about their art, never smile, and having fun doesn't seem to be relevant or important to them. I was talking to one who said he was training so hard for so long that he totally burned out on Aikido. He hated training and needed to take a complete break from it.

Should we not stress the positive goals of compassion and forgiveness, embracing those challenges with an open heart? Descriptions of O-Sensei seem to always talk about his radiance and joy on

the mat. Relaxation and a positive attitude are clearly required to properly extend ki.

Is my expectation of having fun while training in Aikido unrealistic (a materialistic or ego-driven attachment perhaps) or is it an important part of the art? I'm curious what your thoughts are on whether Aikidoists should strive to keep things light and fun, rather than dark and serious. Does it matter?

A. *It looks like you've figured out your own answer, and I agree with it. You mentioned that "Feeling a sense of joy or having fun while training is more of a personal motivator than something required for proper technique." Fun is not only what brings you to the dojo after a hard day at work. Fun is the way we learn. Kittens learn to hunt by playing pouncing and wrestling games. Same for humans. It's driven by an instinct to learn, and by the sheer joy of being alive.*

At another level, O-Sensei said aikido is love. If you don't get joy from experiencing love, then, Buddy, you got trouble. The grim practitioners you describe may not be paying sufficient attention to their practice partners — see the section of my earlier book The Conscious Manager: Zen for Decision Makers *on courtesy, attention, respect and love.*

At still another level, when you are not in an explicit learning situation, e.g. if you are attacked on the street, then the feeling of fun is a luxury you don't have time for. You'll eventually have to examine any attachment to the experience of fun, to advance in Zen martial art. That does not mean giving up fun. If you are practicing with people who really bring you down psychologically, however, you may need to give up practicing with them and find another dojo.

Q. I am also practicing judo. Most of the time, ukes don't resist. They keep their bodies steady and relaxed. Nages try to memorize the steps and tips of each skill. There is not much difference between how aikido and judo practices to this extent.

However, before practices end, judo students do "randori," a kind of competition. Students try to do the skills they learnt, on their opponents. They immediately find how difficult it is to do the skills and throw their opponents to the ground when their opponents really want to counter or defend. Their coach watches the randori and gives comments about how to attack and defend more effectively.

I think it's very good to do randori at the end of practices, trying to move what we learnt from theory to practice, and it makes me improve my skills faster. Aikido lacks this kind of practice. How could our skills really improve if we don't do competition which is more similar to a real fight.

Why don't we do the same thing in aikido practice? If we want to do, how?

A. *Because aikido randori usually involves multiple attackers, it's quite different from judo randori. Randori should be experienced by aikido beginners early on. It's a valuable exercise, teaching strategy, timing, and spatial awareness.*

It need not happen at the end of the practice hour, but could be in the middle!

Importantly, and again in contrast to judo randori, aikido randori is not an occasion to perfect your formal techniques. A full aikido technique takes time — too much time, when another attacker is about to pounce on you. For this reason, as nage you will practice "pass-throughs," moving past the current attacker without

engaging with him, or engaging only minimally. Often in a belt test, Sensei will call randori to a halt when you have separated one of the attackers from the pack, giving you time to execute one, and only one, full clean aikido technique.

If this is not part of your club's current practice, request it of your sensei.

"Competition" is never a part of aikido. Yet you have seen highly skilled senior aikido instructors. So that should answer one part of your question: You can improve without competing.

The other troublesome word in your question is "fight." As a result of your aikido practice, you will use your confidence, your awareness and your harmonizing skills to calm situations that might escalate to violence, or to avoid such situations. Now, I don't believe in unicorns, and I don't believe your skills or mine will forestall all violence. They will, however, reduce the number of attacks you experience, and thus reduce your chances of being injured in an attack, over the course of your lifetime.

If an attack happens, you may resort to aikido technique, but aikido is not "fighting." In particular, your randori experience may help you pass through an attack and run away. No shame in that; you have nothing to prove to some jerk who attacks you.

(Aikido's one-on-one "jiu waza" — free technique — is closer to judo randori, but like any aikido practice, it is not a competition.)

2
Enter the Dojo

◄○►

Aikido teachers urge you to leave your daily cares outside the dojo.

They don't say this just to help you focus on the day's lesson. Any negativity you might bring to aikido practice will infect your classmates, if only in ways subtle and unseen. My early teacher Bill Lee observed, "The vibes travel up and down the mat at the speed of light." Likewise, if a classmate is sad or worried, you will feel an unwelcome darkness affecting your own technique.

By putting your job stresses, family worries, and financial cares aside for an hour's aikido class, you will enjoy a more positive practice, and learn more. You will leave the dojo invigorated and ready to better deal with life's complications.

An old jazz song[3] advises, "Leave your worries on the door-step." Do that when you enter the dojo.

This is another one of those things that's easy to say and hard to do. Believe me when I say it's a habit you can develop over time. Start now.

---

[3] Enjoy a cover of the song at www.facebook.com/celinejazzlady/videos/218244559290454/

3
Big Mind and the Insanity of Attack

◄○►

You have deposited your cares at the dojo door. You enjoy the calm of the practice hall, and perhaps, a moment of meditation before class begins.

When you are calm and not fixated on anything — on any idea, any part of your body, or any object — your awareness is expansive; you are *sane*. You have "big mind."

When someone attacks you, say by grabbing your shoulder, he is fixated on your shoulder. He is showing small mind. He is having a moment of insanity. Of course, trying to attack someone could reasonably be called an act of insanity, anyway.

Your shoulder represents the end of the world to your attacker. The end of your world, in contrast, is infinitely far away, because you have big mind.

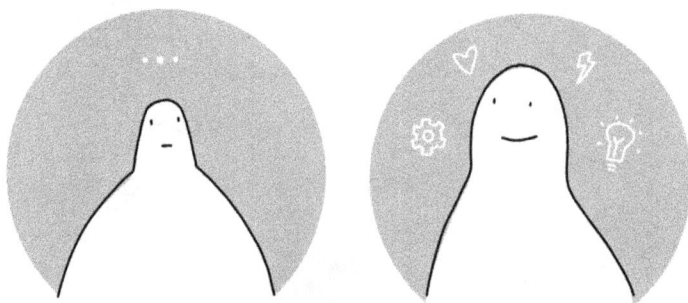

Small mind, Big mind.

You turn tenkan. You have shifted your attacker's balance forward. Your body is no longer blocking his view. In this way you have started to reunite him with big mind. You have started to achieve the *ai* in aikido.

You take him to the ground, more or less painlessly, showing him that the infinite universe does not want the two of you to hurt each other.

4

Escape or Lead?

◄○►

An attacker grabs you. It is easy to break free. Should you try?

Generally, no.

I ask students, What will happen if you break free? They answer rightly that uke can then hit you, kick you, or grab you again.

"Which would you prefer," I ask.

"Oh," a student says, "grab."

"Why?"

"Because it doesn't hurt."

Very sensible. Punches and kicks hurt.

Rather than break free, you will use that point of contact, the grab, to *lead* your uke into an aikido technique.

(Of course if a real attacker grabs you and has a knife in her other hand, you may decide to break free and run for the hills. Use your judgment.)

It's important to see the principle runs both ways, uke to nage and nage to uke. I held the wrists of a nage in kokyu dosa. He pulled in an unnatural direction. I told him, "I almost need to let go of you." Missing the point that he was fighting me and not leading me, he said, "If you let go, I can hit you."

True enough, but in that case I could hit him too. Lead, don't pull.

5
Three Purposes of Tai Sabaki

Your partner attacks you in class practice. You respond. What does your initial tai sabaki (body movement) accomplish?

"Blending," answered one student.

Well yes, but what are the practical aspects of blending?

When responding to an attack from the usual ma-ai, your initial body movement has three purposes: (1) to put you in a place that's momentarily safe from a follow-up attack; (2) to gain control of uke's balance; and (3) to set up for an aikido technique.

Beginners may be able to achieve only one or two of these, but black belts should accomplish all three purposes simultaneously, with a single movement.

More philosophically — but it's a practical philosophy! — we consider that tai sabaki allows nage to "see the world through uke's eyes," a staple aikido principle that helps lead to reconciliation. Nage does this most obviously in the tenkan movement and in what the Iwama folks call the irimi-tenkan tai sabaki. Following these movements, uke and nage are looking in the same direction.

Yet in a direct irimi entry, nage should also feel and share the direction of uke's energy, even lacking a common line of sight. This makes the 1-2-3 of tai sabaki achievable.

6
Tai Sabaki is More Important than Technique

◄◦►

This is simply because if you have completed your initial tai sabaki (see the previous chapter), you can always just push your uke from you, far enough so that you can get a head start as you run away.

Keep this in mind if you suffer a sudden brain freeze and can't remember a full technique. ("Should I do shihonage? Sankyo?")

Naturally this idea is better applied in self-defense than in a rank promotion test, where you are expected to show a technique. But even then, pushing your partner away is better test performance than just stopping and scratching your head. It shows the examiner that you are displaying awareness and zanshin, maintaining your focus between your encounters with uke.

7

Posture is More Important than Tai Sabaki

-◄o►-

Posture is more important, first, before uke contemplates attacking you. Good posture signals that you are not an easy victim, but a person who is aware of your surroundings and able to engage effectively.

Suppose an attack develops anyway, as it always will in a class situation. Second, then, posture is important during tai sabaki. Your purposes in tai sabaki include taking control of uke's balance, that is, his posture. You can hardly do this if your own posture is faulty.

Third, posture is important at the finish of your technique. Though you prefer a gentle finish, and gentle finishes usually suffice, you must be capable of a powerful finish. Power comes from good posture. And in any event, you must finish in a way that leaves you ready for the next attacker. That is, in good posture.

In aikido, you attempt to break your partner's posture to weaken her and allow you to throw her. It's only logical that if your posture as nage is poor, *you* will be weakened, and unable to perform a strong technique.

Upright bipedalism isn't perfect; live long enough, and your hip, knee, or lower back will give you tsuris. Yet we must give nature some credit for evolving us this way. Given that we have just two feet, upright posture gives us the most motive power for the least expenditure of energy.

As your parents told you, stand up straight! Aikido depends on good posture.

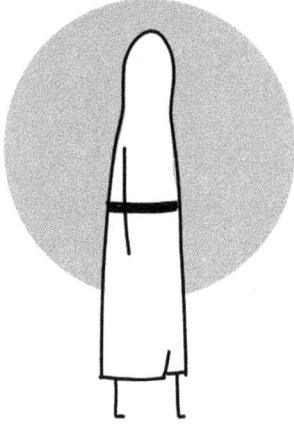

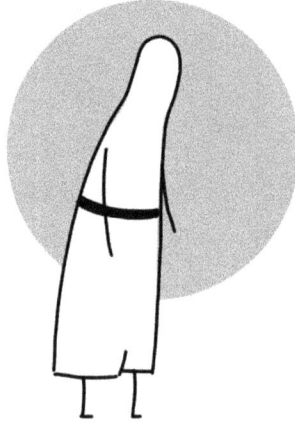

Recommended   **Not recommended**

8
Breath and Ukemi

◄◦►

Do you find forward rolling (mae ukemi) a challenge? Sure, being momentarily upside down can be unpleasant, but that feeling passes quickly, with practice. (A secret: Think "forward" as you roll, not down or up.)

If forward ukemi still makes you queasy, dollars to donuts it's because you're holding your breath. When you round your body to take the forward roll, and do not exhale, the pressure in your innards increases uncomfortably. Many beginning students have unknowingly held their breath while taking forward ukemi, and felt discomfort without realizing why!

Inhale when your body unfolds. Exhale when your body doubles for ukemi. This goes for backward (ushiro) ukemi too.

We don't want students to quit aikido simply because they've forgotten to exhale.

Whenever you're about to roll, make a *whoosh* sound to remind yourself to exhale.

In general, exhale when your body bends forward, and inhale when your body straightens. Aikido will become much more comfortable.

9
Warm-ups

‑‹o›‑

Ichi! Ni! San! Shi! Go! After bowing in and before waza practice, we reach for our left toes five times, then attend to our right toes. Five count for limbering up waist and hips. Then wrists, neck, knees, and ankles.

"Wait," a student objects. "You can't bounce like this in a stretching exercise!"

The student is right. That's why, in most dojos, these are called warm-ups. They are not intended to be stretching exercises. They are gentle movements to activate your muscles and joints.[4]

Your sensei may call the exercises "undo." In Japanese, undo (運動) simply means movement. It does not connote stretching.

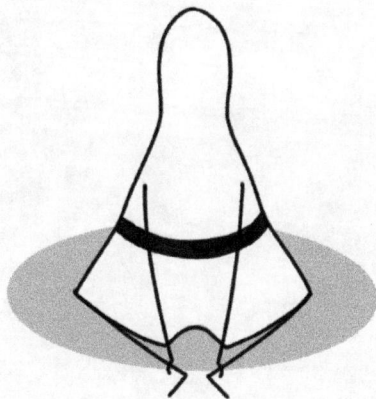

---

[4] The hip-opening undo pictured here put Tohei Sensei in a bawdy mood. "Take care of the lower half of your body," he said. "Someday you may want to use it for something!"

Certainly, stretching exercises can strengthen your body. A flexible body may ease and even improve your aikido practice. If you are motivated to stretch, do it on your own — at home, on the mat before class, or in a yoga studio.

Some aikidoists like yoga as preparation for aikido. Others prefer t'ai chi-type exercises, or any kind of gentle movement that involves the whole body. If the aikido warm-up undo don't satisfy you, you'll find it helpful to add one of the above to your routine.

Though all of us may carelessly say "stretching exercises," and though your sensei may throw in a few true stretches among the warm-ups, stretching is not the main purpose of the aikido warm-ups.

10

Don't Hurry

—◄○►—

Beginning students hurry through a technique, perhaps thinking their partner will be impatient if they take too long. As a result, they don't learn the technique. Don't feel that way — we are all in the dojo to learn, and to help each other learn. Your partner will be patient with you.

Don't dally needlessly, though. If you don't know what to do, don't stand there like a deer in the headlights — try *something*. But take your time.

11

Relax

—◄○►—

Relax completely was one of Tohei Sensei's "four ki principles." "Yeah," his students thought but never had the nerve to say to him, "That's easy for you to say."

Truly, 45 years after taking Tohei Sensei's personal instruction, I am still learning to relax when performing aikido technique. I'm still challenged by the recollection that Tohei did not say, "Relax more." He said, "Relax *completely*." I have no benchmark for this, no experience of what relaxing completely might be like.

Yet relaxation is so important. If uke senses the slightest tension in your arm (or whatever part of you he has grabbed), he'll push back. And your defense technique is aborted.

Thus "relax completely" is related to the other common aikido advice, "Let uke have the part of you that he's grabbed. You can still move everything else."

In repeated class practice, uke's first attack may cause you to tense up. His second attack, even more so, and so on until after several defenses you are just a bundle of accumulated tension, unable to do technique correctly and actually a danger to yourself and to your uke.

To avoid this, check yourself after each throw. As uke is getting up from the mat, you have a moment to feel your shoulders, your eyes, your jaw, your lower back, knees, anywhere you tend to accumulate tension. As best you can, let it go, so you'll feel loose when the next attack comes.

You may have to shimmy and boogie for a second to shake that tension out. Go ahead and do that.

There may be — maybe! — a deeper reason to relax. Fumio Toyoda ridiculed aikidoists who claimed the spirit of Ueshiba O-Sensei guided them through their *dan* tests. "Possessed by O-Sensei, ha!" Toyoda scoffed, "Let the poor man rest in peace." Yet O-Sensei believed the *kami* guided his technique, and that when attacked he left everything to the gods.

Make of that what you will. It's clear though that if you struggle, your struggles are of your own volition. If you relax… then who knows where your movement comes from?

Tohei Sensei allegedly remarked, "The only thing I learned from O-Sensei was to relax." Some students see this as valuable insight. Others (assuming the story and the translation are accurate) think the remark disrespected Ueshiba O-Sensei. I am perfectly uninterested in this argument. Do not write to me about it.

_ RELAX!

12
Changing Your Mind

Exercises like zengo undo, ude furi choyaku undo, and happo giri require you to quickly change the direction of your attention, often by 180 degrees. These are exercises in changing your mind!

"Well," you object, "I frequently change my mind. Some days I change my mind dozens of times. I know how to change my mind!"

Okay, but can you change your mind instantly and completely? Without distraction or pauses for sightseeing as you shift your body and sightline from east to west?

When you apply these exercises in aikido technique, the direction and solidity of your attention make all the difference as regards your solid stance and your ability to throw with the required power.

Practice these aiki taiso as exercises in changing your mind. Your technique will improve.

Because these are attention-switching exercises, the first part of your body to turn the other direction, should be your head (eyes). This is counter-intuitive, because we are trained to initiate most aikido movements with the hips. Turn your head and your attention. Your hips will follow.

13

There is No Tree

—◀◦▶—

When we are startled, our shoulders tense. Our energy flies upward. We lose our grounding, our connection to the Earth, and we say, "You could have knocked me over with a feather."

I believe this reflex is a legacy from our evolutionary ancestors. As our tree-dwelling great-grandpa first descended to the savannah, he was alert to that new environment's danger. At the slightest hint of it, yikes, he jumped back into the tree.

We teach that aikido movements originate from the hips. We cannot turn our hips without pushing with our legs. What do our legs push against? The ground. Effective aikido requires us to stay

Stay grounded.

grounded, conscious of our connection to the ground. More oriented toward the floor beneath our feet than to a tree that might be overhead.

We use the leg push to glide forward, back, left, or right. We rarely jump in aikido technique. We even try not to raise a foot off the ground, but rather to slide. (This is easy on the mat, harder outdoors in rough terrain. And shorter aikidoists do tend to hop, to deal effectively with taller ukes.)

The jump-into-the-tree reflex is our evolutionary inheritance, but it doesn't serve us in aikido. We must remember that in most of our everyday situations, *there is no tree.* We must tell ourselves, and train ourselves, to react to attack by sending that energy not upward, but downward, staying grounded. In this way we keep our balance and our strong posture.

14

Regain the Center

◄○►

In circular aikido techniques, nage wants to stand in the circle's center, and persuade uke to run around its circumference. When I hear, "Sensei, uke's not falling down, please tell us what's going wrong here," often the trouble is that uke and nage are both circling a common center, like the child's "ring around the rosy" game. That way, neither of them has an advantage — in fact, the last line of that nursery rhyme is "*All* fall down!"

Visualize the geometry of *iriminage tenkan*. Nage places herself at the circle's center, her subsequent movement nothing more

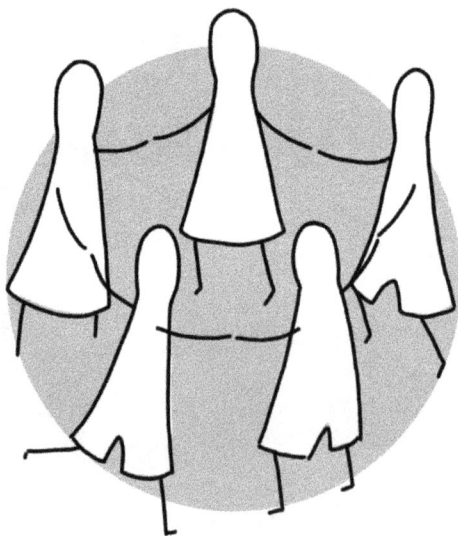

Good fun, but not aikido

than slow pivoting. Uke wears himself out, running around the outside of that circle. Nage draws uke's head toward the circle's center. Uke's feet are now moving faster and farther than his head! Naturally, uke's balance weakens, enabling an easy throw.

As nage, if you find your position has drifted away from the circle's center, take a step to regain the center. It may well make a "difficult" technique easy.

15
Range of Effectiveness

◄○►

When an uke grasps your wrist, your wrist becomes the physical *point of connection* between the two of you. When an uke launches a *mune tsuki* thrust at your belly, you step aside and lay your hand on top of her fist. This touch is your mutual point of connection.

You proceed to tai sabaki and technique. Your technique will be relaxed and powerful when the point of connection is close to your *hara*. If you allow the point of connection to drift close to uke's hara, everything comes to a full stop because that's where uke is strong and you are weak. If your point of connection is midway between uke's hara and yours, no one has advantage. That midway point is the extremity of your range of effectiveness.

In most techniques, you are best served by bringing the point of connection as close as possible to your hara, the center of your range of effectiveness, as soon as possible.

I carefully wrote "physical point of connection" because you have extended your attention to uke, forming a mental connection, even before she launched an attack. If and when an attack ensues, you will form a physical point of connection. Keep it near you.

The point of connection is near uke's center. The advantage goes to uke.

**The point of connection is midway between uke and nage.
Neither uke nor nage has an advantage.**

The point of connection is near nage's center, far from uke's. Advantage nage.

16

Stare at Your Hand, or Stare at the Floor?

◄○►

Neither! How can you maintain big mind if you're staring at hand or floor while attempting a technique?

As much as possible, keep your gaze parallel to the floor, looking "through" the dojo walls, to the ends of the universe.

Have "soft eyes." Too intense a focus will engender tension in the rest of your body, and also inhibit your peripheral vision. Trust your peripheral vision to alert you of dangers.

My teachers would drive these points home with sarcasm: "No need to stare at your hand, it'll probably stay attached to your wrist." "Why are you watching the floor, do you expect it to jump up and bite you?"

It's a similar bad habit, during execution of a technique, to look back at your uke instead of looking where you're going. You become too reactive to uke, when in that situation you must be the boss, the initiator of movement that goes where you want to go while still respecting the limits of where uke can or can't go. Uke is attached to your hand, your wrist, or your shoulder. Body feeling plus peripheral vision will give you all the clues you need about uke's location and trajectory.

17

Around, Not Against

◄◦►

The first time you try to finish an iriminage by pushing against uke's larynx, you'll suspect that "against" is not the right direction. (You'll also annoy your uke, bigtime.) It's an easy lesson. Much harder is to learn what *is* the right direction.

Your teacher may have told you to "follow your fingertips." Wise advice! In iriminage, reach for the corner of the dojo instead of pushing on uke's throat. In sokumen iriminage (also known as sayū nage), your finishing move begins at your belly, as you open your body and arms like a flower in the morning sun. Not pushing on uke's neck or throat.

This is hard to explain in words! Ask your teacher for help, and try directions that are "around and not against."

Left: Nage incorrectly pushes against uke's throat, using arm strength.
Right: Nage opens his torso as he reaches past uke. This is correct, and it changes uke's balance.

There are some directions that a body, when pushed, simply will not move. If your uke doesn't move when you do, he may not be actively trying to stymie you — so don't get upset — he's just showing you that that direction will never work and you should try again, maybe veering a few degrees.

A great many students try to push me in an impractical direction, then say, "Sorry!" I reply, "No sorry, stop with the sorry, we're all here to learn." Rather than spending that moment saying "sorry," spend it thinking about why that direction didn't work. Then too, if you spend an entire class hour apologizing, you'll feel bad about coming to class. We expect students to make lots of mistakes. Give each one a simple "oops," and then try again!

It is also common for a beginner to "push against" in order to finish a technique quickly. If you do this, perhaps it's because you're afraid of wasting your partner's time; you want to keep things moving along. Please get over this fear. You and your partner are both in the dojo in order to learn, and should give each other the time you need to experiment with different finishes. If your uke appears impatient, remind her that she is there to learn, as are you. If that doesn't work, bow to her and go look for a different partner.

(Of course, you're also there to practice ukemi, so keep in mind that if you futz around too long with a throwing technique, you're not getting any falling practice.)

18
Push, Don't Pull

-◄◦►-

It's good to keep the principle "push, don't pull" always in mind.

Test the principle in katate-tori tenkan by entering too shallowly, ending up farther forward than your uke. You will feel you have to yank on uke to get him to move, and it will not work. Without breaking uke's grasp on your wrist, slide-step backward until your arm (the one he is grasping) is more fully extended in front of you. Now you are able to keep "unbendable arm." Moving your hip forward, with your body unified, now allows you to start walking forward, leading your uke.

Left: Nage will finish the tenkan movement still having to pull uke forward. Not effective.
Right: Nage finishes tenkan with his arm extended. See the change in uke's posture.

Likewise, try to finish iriminage when uke's head is behind your shoulder. Tug as you might, uke will not fall, or even move. Back up just a little, enough so that uke's head is in front of you, not behind. Now you can easily complete the throw. See the photos.

You cannot push an uke whose posture you have not first broken. Lead your partner to an untenable posture, and then you may push.

Left: Nage's elbow is behind his shoulder. He is trying to drag uke. Not correct.
Right: Nage's arm is extended and alive. He is pushing, not pulling. This changes uke's posture, making the iriminage easy to finish.

But wait, what about the funakogi (boat rowing) movement? Sure looks like pulling! Yet it isn't. Suppose uke grasps your right wrist, katate tori, starting from standing still, and you execute the ten-shin tai sabaki. This is when you step back and off the line of attack to your left. You must induce uke's motion by using the fune-kogi movement.

In that situation, a nage who is a beginner will tug on uke. A more experienced nage will relax her arm, move her hip back

until the altered angle of uke's grasping hand changes uke's balance, and then simply drop her arm (or make a cutting motion) to initiate a waza.

Okay, that's not pushing. But it's definitely not pulling!

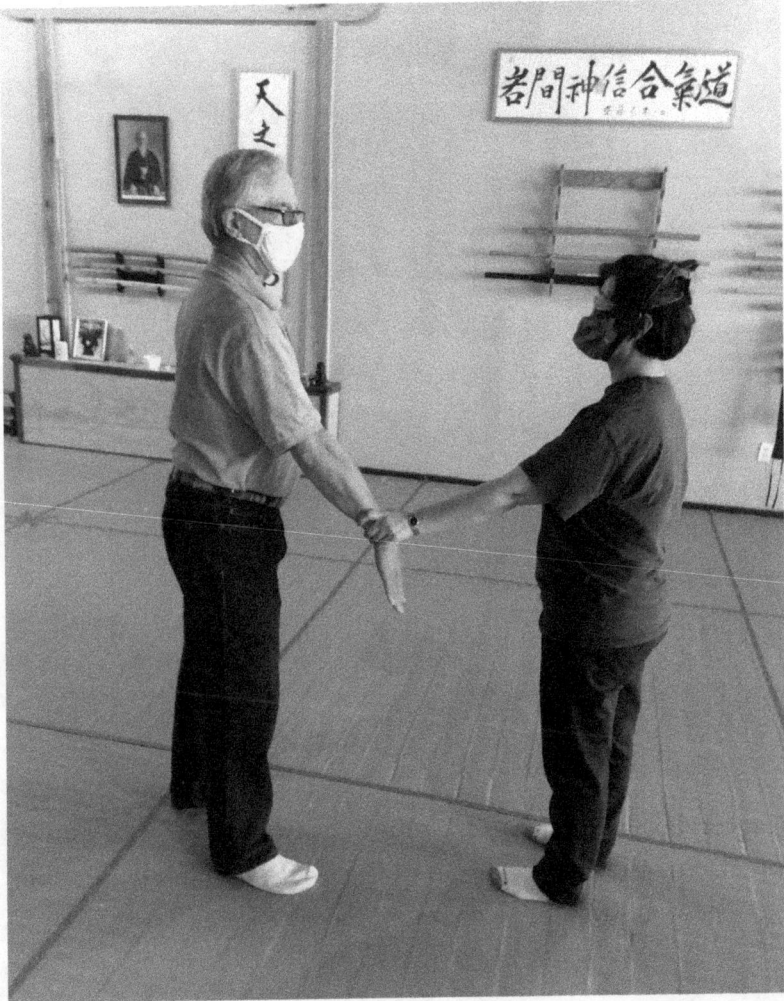

Nage's arm meets uke's at nearly a right angle. Pulling uke will not move her.

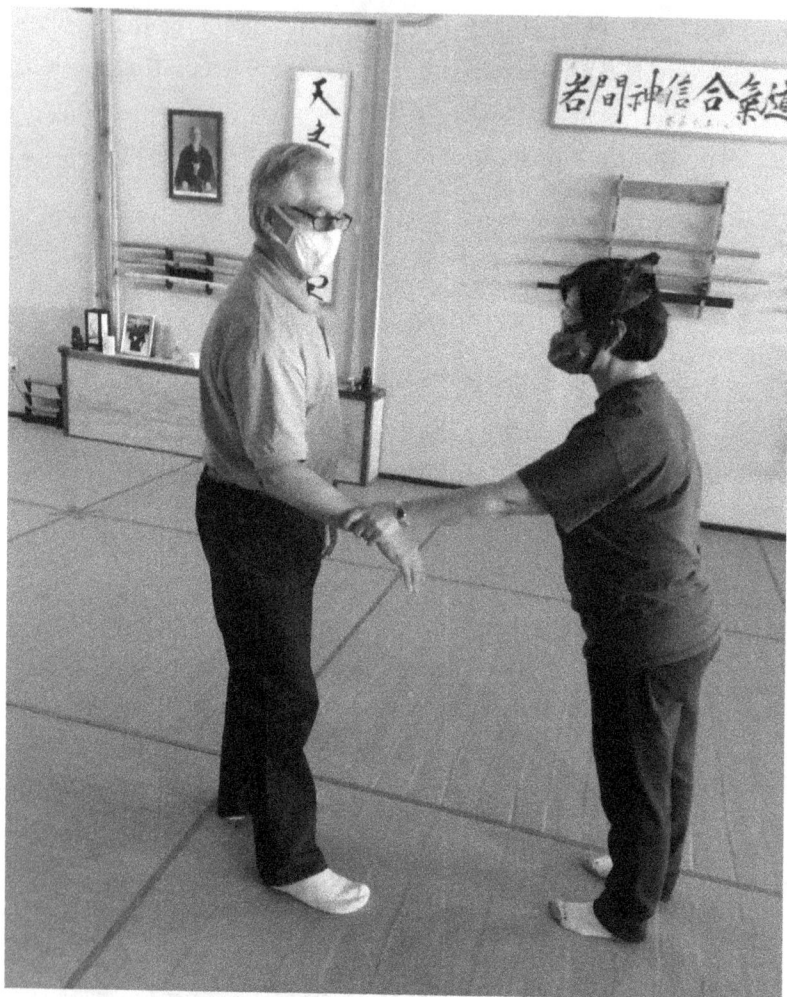

Nage relaxes and drops his elbow, as in the funakogi movement. See the small change in the angle of uke's hand, and the resulting large change in uke's overall posture.

19
Get Close

◄○►

A lot of aikido techniques require close body contact. So why are you standing so far from your uke?

(1) You're shy. (2) The "personal distance" culture in your country dictates that you don't get close. (3) You're afraid your partner will mistake your closeness for an invitation to intimacy. (4) Some other reason that will prevent you from learning the technique.

If you reach too far to contact your partner, you'll lose your balance. Or, you will end up playing ring-around-the-rosy (see the chapter **Regain the center**), and fail to gain the center of the circle that will make technique work.

Are you shy? We don't want to lose you as a student. Talk to your sensei, who may allow you to concentrate for a while on kote gaeshi and other moves that don't require torso-to-torso contact. After a while, you'll feel ready to move from wrist arts to body techniques.

Is it a cultural issue, number two above? In Korea (for example) I've had to stop the class, and have everyone do a five-minute "hugging practice." It worked — I think students were ashamed at the prospect of telling their families that they flunked hugging!

I don't always know what my students do outside the dojo, but I think number three above will not happen. I do recall one occasion when it happened sort of in reverse. I asked Mary (not her real name) to demonstrate full-body ki extension. Two students picked her up and suspended her between two chairs, the edge of one chair under Mary's shoulders and the edge of the other under her ankles. (You've seen stage magicians do this with hypnosis, but no

hypnosis is necessary.) I asked Brad (not his real name either) to sit on Mary's midriff, further demonstrating the strength of her kokyu.

A few weeks later, Brad (who was from Germany) thanked me. He had liked (American) Mary from the start of his practice, he told me, but had been too shy to speak to her. Sitting on her "broke the ice," so to speak, and now they were dating. Some months after, I attended their wedding.

For effective iriminage, kokyunage, koshinage, etcetera… stand close to your partner!

20

Attack Sincerely

◄○►

Uke's attack should give nage enough energy to work with. We don't try to hurt each other in attack-defense practice, of course, but attacks need to be sincere.

This scenario should be familiar: Sensei directs the class to practice a technique from the ryo-kata tori attack. Student "attackers" then trudge toward their nages like sleepwalkers, both arms extended forward. Or Sensei says, "Mune tsuki," and ukes lackadaisically drift toward their nages with one fist extended.

This is aikido practice, not the zombie apocalypse! There's no need to defend against sleepwalkers; nages can ignore these zero-energy attacks and stay perfectly safe. Our aikido principle "enter when pulled, turn when pushed" cannot apply when we are neither pushed nor pulled.

Attack sincerely, with good energy.

How to defend against a zombie attack?
Just walk away.

21
Atemi

◄○►

Your attacker is, most likely, not insane. He has only committed a momentary *act* of insanity, by attacking you. From that moment until you've thrown or pinned your attacker, you mustn't assume he will show further signs of insanity. Assume instead that he will act rationally, even as matters proceed quickly.

Your atemi, then, is not meant to strike your attacker. It sends a "keep away!" message, which a sane *uke* will heed. Nonetheless, you are ready to make a powerful strike if uke shows further insane or suicidal behavior.

(Or masochistic behavior: Jim Harrison, author of *Legends of the Fall*, tells of regretting a thrashing he gave to a man who attacked him in a bar. "Don't worry," the bartender told Harrison, "That guy starts fights because he likes to get beat up.")

Don't think that a person committing an insane act is an insane person. Give ample signal that you're launching an *atemi*. In the dojo, you'll pull your punch for an inexperienced uke.

Outside the dojo, a rational attacker will back off rather than collide with your atemi. An attacker persisting in insanity — or one who is drunk or stoned — will run into your fist. Don't feel bad, if that happens. As a trained aikidoist you have already dealt with this attacker more gently than a fighter would. You have done everything you reasonably can. You are not responsible for another person's acts of insanity.

The police may not believe your "He ran into my fist" story. But that's a different problem!

22
Nerve Techniques and Self-defense

Sensei tells the class to practice tenchinage. "Great," you think, because you can keep throwing and falling tenchinage 'til the cows come home. Sensei claps and changes the practice to yonkyo. You take yonkyo ukemi six times, and your wrists are begging, "Please! No more!"

Every nage likes to find uke's radial nerve, and knuckle it to lend extra pizazz to yonkyo. It's fun — sort of.

Sensei might place a knuckle under your jaw, catching the lingual or mylohyoid nerve to add a little something to her iriminage. (Hint: If you're a tough guy, disguise your cry of pain as a *kiai*.) Your next partner may apply nikkyo or sankyo in a painful way.

Ouch!
Owww!
Ouch!

Hii-yaaa!

It's good to know how to apply painful techniques. It's better not to depend on them. This is simply because in a self-defense situation, an attacker who is drunk, stoned, or even really angry will not feel pain. You might apply a forceful sankyo to such a person with no seeming effect, until his wrist breaks — and even this will not stop him.

Depend instead on leading your attacker, with technique that takes uke's joints in directions they naturally go — unarguably must go — and controls uke's posture. Ikkyo does this, for example: We almost never apply nerve pressure in that technique. Yonkyo works perfectly well if you hold uke's forearm like a sword, imagine the tip of the sword is the top of uke's head, and cut. No nerve pressure is needed.

Learn both ways! Know the nerve techniques, but depend on the leading techniques.

Attend also to the randori pass-through, or "bye-bye" movements. (See the chapter "**Q&A: Aikido and martial art practice**.") When you have passed through the attack of an intoxicated belligerent and are no longer in his field of vision, he may just completely forget about you.

23
Kumitachi Make No Sense. Practice Them Anyway

—◄o►—

Sensei: You'll lose your fingers if you grip the bokken blade! Pretend it's sharp!

Student: Uh, hai, Sensei!

Sensei: On number 3 you must strike yokomen uchi!

Student: But Sensei, you said on #1 you sliced open my intestines. How can I...

Sensei: Yeah, okay, pretend I missed on #1. Gimme a yokomen!

Then between movements number 3 and 4, you see an easy opening. You remember the maxim of famed swordsman Yamaoka Tesshu:

Don't hold back,
Trying to protect your ass;
As soon as an
Opening appears,
Seize it !

You could stick your partner right through the gizzard! But the kata does not recognize this option. Sensei yells, "That's not number 4!" You must proceed with #4 as prescribed. You think, "This is no way to learn to sword fight!"

The kumitachi set-pieces leave us unsure what we're supposed to treat as real, what we're supposed to pretend, and what we should ignore.

The thing to understand is that kumitachi are only indirectly about self-defense. Kumitachi is not about learning to win a sword fight. If you were to try these aiki-ken moves against a katori-ryu practitioner, she would slice you into sashimi!

Kumitachi is about learning precise body positioning and angles, and about coordinating your movement with a partner's. It's about learning not to panic and overreact when someone swings a stick at your head. It's about learning to extend your attention through the weapon and beyond, feeling as if it is part of your body. You'll gain insights about these things beyond what you gain from unarmed practice, and these will increase your self-defense abilities.

Aikido instructors do not realistically expect you to find yourself in a sword fight. Don't think that kumitachi will prepare you for one. And yet, as Tesshu continued,

Do not think that
This is all there is.
More and more
Wonderful teachings exist.
The sword is unfathomable.

24
You Will Do Aikido With Your Mind

-◄o►-

Changing your mind changes your body. Koichi Tohei Sensei often said this. His "extend ki" exercises amply demonstrated it. For example, if you think "down" when you are pushed from the front, you will stand solid; if you think "up" in that same situation, you'll be pushed over.

In aikido technique a mind focused in the correct direction makes the difference between a strong technique and uke running away with you.

In a promotion test, examiners may ask you for technique after technique, just to tire your body, so they can see whether your mind and your will can continue to do aikido.

I learned this lesson not in a test but in a visit to Japan. An old friend took me to a class at Honbu Dojo in Tokyo. In a strenuous class in America I would not hesitate to rest in seiza for a few moments at the side of the mat. But of course one is embarrassed to do that at Honbu Dojo, so I continued, beyond physical exhaustion but with mind still present. My friend, then close to 250 pounds, came in for attack. My legs refused to move. We were both surprised that he simply bounced off me and found himself three or four steps away, while I had moved not an inch. "Hmm," he remarked, "You've been practicing."

That wasn't quite the right explanation, but I was too bemused and too tired to argue.

Do you use your body in aikido? Of course! Yet the relation between your mind and body is an essential element of your advancement.

See the chapter on **Intention**, later in this volume.

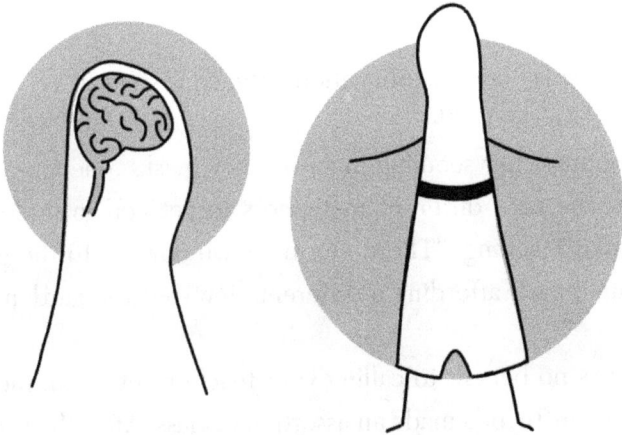

Mind and body together

25

I Say Same, You Listen Different!

◄○►

Your teacher is under no obligation to be consistent. It's confusing, though, when she isn't!

Sometimes her seeming inconsistency masks a deeper consistency, as she tries different metaphors to get you to understand a particular teaching. "There are many windows onto the garden of learning, each affording a different view, but the garden is the same."

There's no benefit to calling your teacher out on an inconsistency. Shihan Toyoda made an assertion in class. After the practice, I asked him, "But Sensei, last year you said (something that seemed to me to be the opposite)."

His stern retort was, "I say same, you just listen different!"

Thought-provoking the man was.[5]

Maybe Toyoda was saying, look deeper, and maybe he was saying, hey, just learn to live with contradiction. In any case, his new assertion showed that the way he explained it the previous year wasn't working for the class, so he tried a new way.

Or maybe he was right, and it was I who had changed.

Confronting him about it did nothing but embarrass both of us.

---

[5] That Star Wars style sentence is a tribute to Toyoda. We used to tease him that if he were to lose the first part of his name, he would be "Yoda."

26
Your Teacher and Your Aikido Organization

—◄◊►—

In the book's Introduction, I mentioned my personal "teaching emphasis." Each teacher teaches with his or her own emphasis. We all teach the curriculum required by our respective aikido organizations (which are sometimes called "federations"), but the tone and theme of one teacher's class are usually quite different from those of another teacher in the same federation.

In fact, the differences between two teachers in the same federation might strike you as bigger than the average difference in teaching styles between federations.

What this should tell you is that you should choose a teacher whose teaching emphasis "speaks" to your learning style.

You do not need to like your teacher. After all, you probably remember a teacher in high school who — you now realize — inspired you but whom you absolutely detested. The aikido teacher-student relationship is one of mutual respect, not necessarily one of friendship.

As your aikido grows over a period of years, you may find that your teacher's teaching doesn't speak to you anymore. You will then find a new teacher. Your old teacher, I hope, demands your respect but not your loyalty; she will not be offended if you go. However, your decision to leave should never be made lightly.

A teacher's style and emphasis depend on his personality, his circumstances, and what he has taken from studying the art for many years. It's good that a teacher's aikido is infused with

personality: If your teacher is a pure technician, you'll be too bored to return to his class. This statement's flip side should be obvious: If the dojo is a sensei's "personality cult," you'll be unlikely to learn much aikido.

And another caution: Ueshiba O-Sensei's own teaching evolved during his lifetime. His students in the 1940s learned, and passed along, techniques and ideas that differed from what his 1960s students took away. O-Sensei's later lectures were notoriously incomprehensible. Thus, if you meet teachers (as I have) who claim that they are teaching the true technique of O-Sensei and that other teachers are in error, you should be, at the least, very skeptical.

27
Should I Ask for a Test? Should I Take a Test If Asked?

◄○►

If your dojo-cho does not keep close track of class attendance, or if most classes are taught by assistant instructors, or if you are running a branch dojo, your sensei may not be aware of your progress or the hours you've put in since your last test. In those cases, you should feel free to remind your sensei of these facts and ask for a test.

Actually, the only test I ever asked for was sandan. The dialog went something like this.

Fred: Sensei, it's been a long time. May I have a test?
Toyoda: I hardly ever see you. Why should I test you?
Fred: Since I moved to Texas I have been teaching regular classes there as you directed, and I come back to Chicago to see you whenever I can. I've attended most of your seminars, and hosted you twice in Austin.
Toyoda: Yeah, that's right, you have. OK, take test.

All my other tests and promotions have been by invitation, and unexpected. As I implied in the Preface, I felt ridiculously unready for my shodan test. My feeling proved right, though the eventual outcome was positive. One of the plus outcomes is that I learned "Who, me?" is never the right answer when you are invited to test. The right answer is always, "Hai, Sensei! I'll do my best!"

So when your sensei tells you it's time to take a test, say "Hai, Sensei!" Then do your best, during the test and in the months and years after. Tsutomete! (That means "try hard"!)

Aside from your own advancement, there's an element of "dojo duty" in taking a test. You become a sempai, and your juniors in class (kohai) know they may look to you for help.

Then too, a test is an alternate kind of learning experience, different from an ordinary class. Don't shun tests, they are good for you — even if you fail. However, your teacher will not ask you to test unless she is quite sure you are ready.

Treat an invitation to test not as a reward for accomplishments to date, but as Sensei's gesture of confidence in your potential for future growth.

Say, "Hai, Sensei!"

28
Postscript

─◄○►─

Okay, I cannot leave the story untold, after dropping so many hints. Rod Kobayashi Sensei kindly avoided the word "fail" after my execrable shodan test. Instead, he said, "We'll have 'Test, Part 2' when I see you this summer."

Come summer, I spent two weeks with him at Tom Crum's camp in Aspen, Colorado, thinking, "When's the test?" but knowing it would be impolite to ask.

Near the two weeks' end, I had donned my hakama (Sensei encouraged 1st kyus to wear hakama), headed for the mat, then reversed course, thinking it wise to take a last-minute pee before the morning class. At the urinal, I hiked up one side of the hakama, reached underneath to untie the gi pants, pulled them partly down, and commenced my business.

A gnome's head appeared around the partition separating urinals. It belonged to the 4'11" Kobayashi Sensei, who startled me good. He said, "Ah, Phillips, so you've learned the secret."

That afternoon he formally handed me a shodan certificate.

Three Austin friends were with me in Aspen, in cahoots with Rod Kobayashi in the certificate caper. Thus, I had to live this down, as well as live up to it.

So there it is: Urinating without removing hakama might get you promoted. Good luck with it.

Subsequent tests were odd in their own ways, but none reached the comedic peak of the shodan test.

29
Out of the Dojo

—◁o▷—

In your dojo, even when your uke is attacking you, you should feel safe. Feeling safe helps you relax. Relaxation, in turn, helps you do technique effectively.

If you are attacked on the street, that feeling of safety is absent, and in fact you are not safe! Especially if the attack surprises you, your attempt at aikido technique is likely to be somewhere between seriously degraded and totally crappy.

How to prepare?

In his youth, Toyoda Sensei and his friends would go to bars and provoke fights, to test their abilities in "real" situations. I do not recommend this! Though I know some of you youngsters are going to do it anyway.

Alternatives are:

➤ Aikido practice — especially *randori* — develops your awareness. Being aware of your physical surroundings is great self-defense. Don't walk down that alley, but take the well-lighted street instead. If you see aggressive-looking people, position yourself to make it hard for them to surround you. Relax your eyes and trust your peripheral vision. It can alert you to danger.

➤ Your awareness will extend to situations as well as locales. You'll feel the vibes as people around you become agitated. Time to leave the room! If violence erupts, you'll be elsewhere.

➢ As an aikidoist you are able to see the world through your attacker's eyes. You'll perceive what's bothering him and you're able to talk him down. You are confident but you have nothing to prove; the thought "I can take this guy" will never tempt you.

Don't walk around with your nose buried in your smartphone. Carry a "mugger wallet," an old billfold containing a few dollars and an expired credit card; if you are mugged, throw it to the ground and run.

The social media offer plenty of (mostly ill-informed) chatter on whether aikido techniques are effective on the street, or against the methods of other martial arts. There is also plenty of (much better) writing about bringing aikido principles of harmony etc. to daily life.

The items of advice I've given you in this chapter don't seem to appear in other books or media. I think they are the best ways to deal with potential physical conflict outside the dojo. They won't keep you safe 100% of the time. But they will get you through many a trying situation.

Practice randori!

30
Play Your Own Game

-◄◦►-

Years ago, a promoter pitted champion boxer Muhammad Ali against a pro wrestler before an audience of thousands. It was boring. The wrestler dropped to the mat and invited Ali to grapple. Too canny for that, Ali beckoned the wrestler to stand and exchange blows. The smart wrestler wouldn't comply. To sum up, nothing happened.

Even worse, the lesson didn't take. You can find YouTube videos in which an aikidoist enters a cage with an MMA fighter and gets trounced. This doesn't reflect badly on aikido, only on the intelligence of that aikidoist.

A sure way to get beat up is to play the other guy's game, a game in which he is expert and you are not. Stick to your own game, your own expertise, and don't be drawn into the opponent's game.

No need to be rigid in your approach. Do what you need to do in order not to match your attacker blow for blow. If the attacker seems wild and crazy, you must project focus. If the attacker is focused, you can project wild and crazy. (The Chinese "drunken master" movies wonderfully illustrate this.) Either way, you are still an aikidoist, so act like one.

Indeed, if "nothing happens," that is the best possible outcome.

31
Practice!

◄○►

Don't let aikido esthetics distract you, though aikido is beautiful. Practice!

Don't let aikido philosophy distract you, though it is profound. Eventually you will embody it. Meanwhile... practice!

Don't let aikido spirituality distract you. It will come to you in time. For now... practice!

Don't let aikido rank promotions distract you. Help your kohai to learn, and let them help you practice!

Know some aikido history — it is magnificent, and it creates what you are and what you will be — but don't let it distract you. You're here to become an aikidoist, not an historian. Practice!

Don't let aikido personalities distract you. As a yudansha you will develop your own aikido personality. Practice!

Don't get caught up in talking about aikido. Practice!

Aikido friendships are wonderful. True aikido friends will encourage your practice!

Balance thinking about aikido ("mental practice") with physical practice.

Oh, did I mention? Practice!!!

ESPECIALLY FOR TEACHERS

32

Motivating Beginners

—◁◦▷—

Beginners are not just learning new movements, but a whole new mode of body movement. It may take time. Give them all the time they need, warning them only that repeatedly hurting their partners will lead to ejection from the dojo.

Some beginners find aikido's complex movements discouraging. Others take them as a fascinating challenge. To keep the first group motivated,

➢ Demonstrate a variety of techniques to the class but allow a diffident student to stick with practicing one technique for an extended period of time.

➢ Teach Tohei Sensei's elementary *ki* principles, which don't require any movement at all.

➢ Emphasize how important it is for the student's life, to know how to fall down safely, even if she never masters another aikido technique.

As a beginner I was a member of the second group. I just *had to* understand why my teacher could execute the katate-tori tenkan movement and I could not. A teacher can leverage these second-group people by pairing them for practice, letting them infect the first group with their enthusiasm.

Knowing that in my twenties I was a slow learner of physical skills, I was inspired to find out that Ueshiba O-Sensei practiced

into his mid-80s. I thought, hmm, by the time I'm 80, I can be really good at this! It's still my goal, and I've made encouraging progress toward it. The portrait on the shomen of O-Sensei in his eighties constantly reminds me of it. I suppose the lesson for teachers is, devote yourself to students according to their devotion to aikido, not according to their speed of learning.

Give sincere and complete answers to beginners' questions, no matter how silly they may seem. If a beginning student shows an interest in aikido history, or Japanese language (as one of my successful students did), indulge his interest, while emphasizing that regular class attendance and physical practice are the true keys to progress in aikido.

If beginners seem fascinated with the beauty of aikido movements, the philosophy of responsible pacifism, or the dojo ritual, these can be the hooks that keep them practicing. As the earlier chapter "**Practice!**" shows, students eventually will have to become un-fascinated by these things, concentrating instead on practicing their aikido. As their teacher, you can guide this transition.

Flashy demonstrations are inspiring, but a newbie may think, "If Sensei's gonna make me take those big falls, I'm outta here." Explain to beginners that they will not be taking big breakfalls until and unless they feel ready.

33
Fear of Falling

◄◐►

"Mat, this is Student. Student, say hello to mat." After this silly but effective introduction, ask the beginning student to sit on the mat, pat the mat, bounce around a little, and make friends with the mat. This will make an introduction to ukemi easier. It will never do for the student to think of the floor as something to be frightened of.

The beginner learns forward ukemi first from a kneeling position. You may use one hand to protect his head as he takes his first forward roll, and the other hand to push on his rear ankle, for momentum. Push the ankle, not the buttocks! The latter, while more efficient for the purpose, is too intimate — and depending on the jurisdiction, probably illegal. Convey this warning to all advanced students who are teaching ukemi to newcomers.

Later a student will take her first ukemi from shihonage. Just before the fall she will find her back is arched — a particularly scary stance from which to fall. Remind the student not to feel frozen in the arched position; she may deliberately drop her bottom, assuming a near-squatting position from which she may take the fall smoothly and gently.

Most dojos teach forward and backward rolls, moving on to variations of these, forgetting the "front splat" fall that ends, for example, the ikkyo takedown. It is wise to devise an exercise that introduces the student to the front splat, before their first ikkyo surprises them with it!

34

Zen Conversations

‑◄◦►‑

You may have heard that aikido technique is a *conversation* between uke and nage. This is another way of saying that in aikido, uke is not a passive paper target on the firing range, or a wooden *wing chun* dummy. Uke is a human being who will do unexpected things to protect herself during the seconds it takes to complete a technique. The conversation consists of "I try to do this, but uke does that, so I will adjust thusly, and see what uke does next."

My own teachers didn't use the word "conversation," but took a more Zen approach — basically, don't have any expectations, then you'll be instantly able to adapt to anything.

I've seen danger in the "conversations" way of teaching. It entices nage to *expect* uke either to cooperate too much with a technique or to attempt to counter it. As a result, nage never learns to do a complete technique correctly. As one Facebook post put it, nages "short-change the move they are doing for the move they are going to do next."

Certainly uke may sometimes attempt to counter. Better that teachers devote occasional classes exclusively to kaeshi waza and henka waza. Then students have the opportunity both to learn solid technique and to adapt fluidly.

35

Atemi 2: The Force Continuum

◄○►

The law allows you to defend yourself. In many jurisdictions, the law does not allow you to respond to attack with a level of force significantly higher than the attacker used. My non-lawyer interpretation of this is, if you are in a fistfight, you may end it by threatening your unarmed opponent with a knife, but you may not actually cut him with it unless he persists in striking you.

In the self-defense situation, when we respond to an attacker's unarmed grasp or thrust, we may execute ikkyo. Generally we prefer to roll uke's elbow rather than break it. Uke then takes a forward fall, his arm remaining uninjured.

If an attacker on the street is armed, we should run away! But if we can't, we can respond to a thrust with gokyo, in which uke's meeting with the ground is not so gentle. Or we do a variant of sokumen iriminage, with an elbow to his nose. If we face many armed attackers, we may break the arm of the first knife fighter, in order to more advantageously face the others.

Students may like or dislike aikido's initial appearance of gentle sweetness and light. Either way, they should eventually be told that aikido *allows* them to be gentle, but also allows them to escalate their response force as the situation demands and as the law allows.

36
Eye Contact in Aikido

At a dojo in Beijing, a student asked, "Should I look into uke's eyes?" Here's how the question came about. Most defenses from yokomen-uchi start with nage's arms extending toward uke in the manner of *shomen-uchi ikkyo undo*. A nage's common mistake is to raise the arms toward uke's attacking hand.

There's nothing an attacker loves more than to have you distracted by that hand! He'll then move in with his other hand and punch your lights out. As nage, your problem is uke — not uke's hand. You must raise your hands directly toward uke's face while executing the ten-shin tai sabaki.

Beginners find it hard to believe that this will protect them from the yokomen attack. Trying it, they will quickly see that it does.

Okay, now suppose the defense is to be nikkyo. Nage continues with an ikkyo-type motion, causing uke to bend 'way over. Then nage will do something quite dangerous, namely, allow uke to stand up again. (This is a formalism of the nikkyo technique. You would not want to do it in a self-defense situation, unless there was a strategic reason for doing so. After all, where you ultimately want uke to be is on the ground.)

Here is where eye contact comes in. By the time uke comes upright, nage must be already in a firm posture, uke's hand nestled into the hollow of the shoulder, and looking into uke's eyes. As nage, you have allowed uke to return to a standing position, but you must be there first, and you must make it clear to uke that *you are the boss*.

Otherwise, the nikkyo technique is much too dangerous for nage. It allows uke to regain the initiative.

(Aikido is a Japanese art, and in Japanese culture one may make direct eye contact only with a subordinate, a spouse, or a lover. When your Japanese sensei throws you, she may look into your eyes because as a student you are subordinate. When throwing Sensei, you should imitate your sensei's other technical moves, but not that one!)

In the case of yokomen defense, raise your arms toward uke's face. Don't look into uke's eyes. People are good at using their eyes to fake their intentions. Football players are taught to look at the opposing linemen's hips, not their eyes, for just this reason. That's good advice for aikidoists too.

However, for nikkyo, yes, you want to look into uke's eyes. This is not amorous. When O-Sensei said the essence of aikido is love, he meant universal love, not l'amour! Eye contact in nikkyo is primate dominance behavior. It says, *I am the boss!*

In aikido, such behavior is an exception. Aikido's purpose is not to establish dominance. Our purpose is to learn more and more about peaceful coexistence and mutual respect. Every system has exceptions, though. In aikido we do not make direct eye contact, except in nikkyo, or in other henka waza in which we allow uke to momentarily regain upright posture.

Or, if we are flirting with our partner!

37
Unifying and Separating

◄○►

In many and perhaps most aikido movements, the body must be unified. In katatetori tenkan, for example, nage cannot succeed by moving her trunk and her arm separately. Her trunk and limbs move together (with *kokyu*, or *ki* extension) so that the force of her legs against the floor can be transmitted efficiently to uke.

Now imagine you are resting your arms on a bridge railing, and the railing suddenly collapses. If your body is unified, you'll be resting all your weight on the railing, and you will fall into the river. If your posture is solid, you may *separate* — allowing your arms to fall to your sides — without your body falling. This saves your life, or at least, keeps you dry.

This is separation. It is useful. You have "taken a load off" by resting the weight of your arms on the railing; your legs and trunk, for a few moments, don't have to bear the weight of your arms. Yet you have protected yourself by not making your posture dependent on the railing.

In fact if you lean on the railing with body unified, you are probably holding up your body with your arms, not very restful. Or — funny image — if the railing goes and your body and arms remain where they were, arms now suspended in mid-air, you were not really resting them on the railing at all.

Be aware of unification and separation, and when to use each. A few applications in ukemi are obvious: If you attack with a weapon and nage defends, when should you let go of the weapon and take

your fall? (As the chapter on Kumitachi noted, we are encouraged to think of the weapon as an integral part of our body.) When you grab nage's body, when should you then let go, in order not to take a dangerous fall, or not to have your wrist broken?

When uke grabs your arm, you "let him have your arm" as you move your body to an advantageous position. This might involve "separating" your arm for a moment, so as not to send resistance signals to uke. You'll then continue the movement with body unified.

How to apply the unify/separate principle in other aikido situations is left as an exercise for the reader.

At the gym, a weightlifter grimaces as he jerks a barbell. You wonder, does this guy think he can lift it *with his mouth?* Maybe he could relax his mouth and redirect the energy to lift even more weight. Our weight-lifting gym-mate has failed to *separate* his facial muscles from his lifting muscles, when doing so would benefit him.

Readers might know that "separation" can mean a slight dislocation of a joint. Though this chapter uses the same word, I mean "separation" in a non-medical sense, namely, a deliberate suspension of *kokyu* that allows you to move one part of your body while leaving another part a little bit behind.

This principle, too, stems from Koichi Tohei's teaching. It is similar to a yoga teacher's instruction to "isolate" a particular muscle or set of muscles.

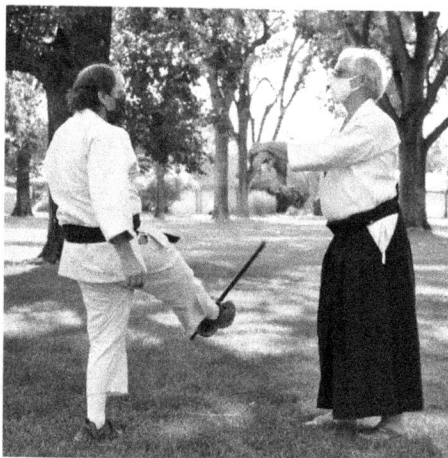

Left: Nage rests his arms atop the jo.
Right: Nage's body was balanced but inappropriately unified, leaving his arms suspended, ridiculously, when uke kicks the jo aside. Nage was not resting his arms!

Here, nage was unified but unbalanced, meaning he relied on the jo for his posture and fell when the jo was removed.

When uke kicks the jo aside (it is on the ground on lower left), nage's arms drop in a relaxed manner. His torso is unaffected. This demonstrates correct separation.

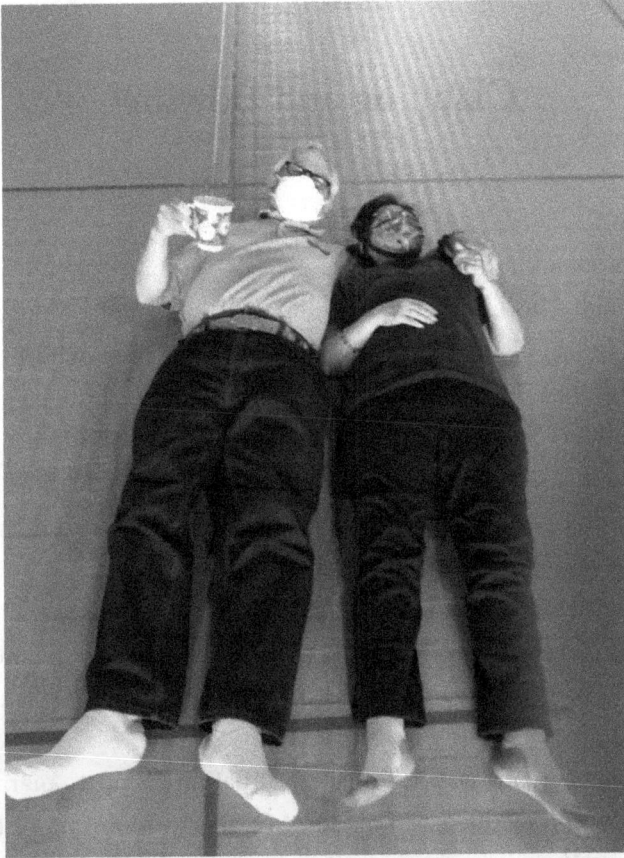

A non-aikido application of this chapter's principle.
The lady is sleeping on the gentleman's shoulder. He
wishes not to disturb her as he sips his coffee. To do this,
he must "separate" his left arm, leaving it relaxed while he
exercises his coffee muscles.

38
Clapping and Bowing

◄o►

Have an open mind.

Though Ueshiba O-Sensei followed the Omoto Shinto sect, he selected as his technical successor Koichi Tohei, whose family were Buddhist. Tohei Sensei was instrumental in bringing aikido to the United States, a decidedly non-Shinto, non-Buddhist country. Though aikido's antecedents lie deep in Japanese culture, most early aikido teachers believed aikido to be a universal art that could benefit anyone, of any belief, in any country.

(Or at least, they admirably and conscientiously separated the bits that would benefit foreigners from the untranslatable bits that had to do with Japanese nationalism and the subtleties of samurai culture.)

During the postwar American occupation of Japan, martial art practice was forbidden to Japanese. O-Sensei represented to the Americans that the goings-on at Tokyo's Honbu Dojo were little more than calisthenics. He banished rough-and-tumble martial practice to Iwama, in the countryside, where the military occupiers wouldn't notice. No schism in aikido theory or practice was contemplated; this was just a way of keeping aikido going during the occupation years.

Though the separations from Honbu of Tomiki aikido, Ki Society, etc. were painful to those involved, no one argued that aikido, in any of these schools, was anything other than the martial art of harmony, blending, and reconciliation.

Maybe a different teaching emphasis, but not a different art, and certainly not a religion!

Schools in some aikido lineages maintain that "What we do is different." Well, teaching-style differences between schools might confuse a beginner, and test-art requirements may differ, but to an experienced practitioner, aikido is aikido.

When students travel

Recognizing this, some teachers encourage students to experience a wide range of inputs, by taking classes from different teachers, by traveling, etc. These experiences enrich the students' learning, and I applaud their open-minded teachers.

Still other teachers demand "loyalty" from their students and forbid visits to other dojos. I find it sad that such teachers are so insecure about their skills or their income, that they would treat students this way.

Ritual

Vince Salvatore Sensei remarked that some new arrivals at his Reno dojo are put off by the ritual clapping (a Shinto thing) and bowing (a Japanese thing) at the opening and close of each class.

Apropos of this, years ago a prospective student phoned me. He asked, will aikido violate his Christian beliefs? I replied, certainly not. He persisted, "But you meditate." I noted that I believe Christians meditate, too. He opined that the practice was a heretic "oriental" influence on Christianity. I tried again, saying many people think Jesus spent his "missing years" in India. His reply? "Only Jesuits think so!" Clearly this was a man who wanted to divide people and beliefs into smaller and smaller slices, and reject everyone

not in his slice. I would have done my best for him had he joined my class, and maybe he eventually would have taken on a broader outlook. But I confess I'm glad he didn't join.

To honor O-Sensei's memory, as religious views divide Americans and as aikido "lineages" continue to splinter, aikido really must remain the universal art of peace, welcoming students of all religions. It is a force for uniting, not for dividing. Any physical technique that blends with an attack, effectively protects nage, and causes no unnecessary harm to uke, is an aikido technique — no matter which school teaches it.

A hand-clap may mean something specific and spiritual to a Shinto adherent. I don't much care. If a dojo-cho wants to clap while bowing in, I'll join him or her, as a way of showing respect for the art of aikido as I've describe it above, for the dojo it is practiced in, and for the founder's memory.

39

Slow Time

◄◦►

Michael Cusumano and David Yoffie published an article on "Judo Strategy and Internet Time" in *Harvard Business Review*. From their title, you would figure they're saying everything has to happen faster. You do have to comb the article carefully to find their warnings that managers should not persist in fast movement just for movement's sake or if it causes a loss of focus; and that quickness can't substitute for quality.

Indeed, we usually associate speed with quantity, and slowness (slow dancing, slow-cooked barbecue, etc.) with quality. Business can't be all speed. Like an aikido technique, it has natural beats of quickness and slowness.

Perhaps parochially, I find aikido a richer source of metaphors for business than judo. Judo is usually taught as a tournament sport, meaning (i) it has rules, (ii) bouts are of a fixed duration, and (iii) when it's over, there's a winner and a loser. In business it's never over, and a winner/loser mentality is limiting. None of the three features of sport judo are true for aikido, or for business.

When attacked, an aikidoist's response often has three phases. The first, "tai sabaki," is fast. It places the defender in a position that is both momentarily safe from follow-up attack, and advantageous for a takedown or throw. Second is the setup, leading the attacker to an unrecoverable posture. The setup is usually slow, because the defender is in the middle of a circle and can revolve in an almost leisurely way while the attacker must travel the circle's circumference on increasingly difficult footing. (Uke's circular path

also serves as a "defensive perimeter" that keeps additional attackers away from nage for the moment.) Third is the finish, which is fast so the defender can turn her attention to other attackers. More complex techniques involve repositionings that make for additional beats of slow and fast.

In aikido we believe "if you can't do it slow, you can't do it fast." This means that new students who attempt to do techniques fast (on all the beats) will never learn the control, energy flow and finesse that will make aikido work against an attacker who is even bigger, stronger and faster. Nor will they develop a philosophical framework that will help them understand what they know and what they don't know.

Aikido is Zen martial art. Students may sit zazen as part of the training, and thereby realize that "time isn't all it's cracked up to be." After all, do we sit fast or do we sit slowly?

So an aikido technique is made of beats of time. During some of those beats you attend to uke's balance and placement. During other beats you check your own posture. During still others, you need to pay attention — without staring at it! — to the point of connection between the two of you, whether wrist, shoulder or other. I know of no way to write down how to do this. Simply be conscious of it when practicing.

40

Empathy and Martial Art

-◄◦►-

National Public Radio highlighted a study showing that Americans are 40% less empathetic than 20 years ago. The decline includes empathic characteristics like compassion, and the ability to see from another person's perspective.

Hmm. Compassion and perspective shift are what aikido is all about. How can we "see the world through uke's eyes," for example via the tenkan movement, without a certain amount of empathy?

Pundits have attributed aikido's declining enrollments in America to the rising popularity of mixed martial arts. The NPR report implies aikido's decline is not solely due to MMA, but to decreased general empathy. (It gave no clue as to whether MMA is a cause or an effect of declining empathy.)

Happily, not all young people exemplify empathic decline. My daughter, having rejected Dad's synagogue and Mom's church, was thrilled to meet the Dalai Lama, and thinks His Holiness' simple message of compassion is all she needs to get through life. She has remained true to the message, with much success in her professional and family life.

The study reported on NPR was a longitudinal meta-analysis of empathy studies, using well-accepted psychological scales. It may help us understand how to bring more young people into aikido.

My dance teacher concisely characterized people who are open to learning tango: "Highly intelligent, with slightly addictive personalities." How would you describe the psychology of potential aikido students?

41
Learning Styles

◄○►

If you teach a variety of movements, students' body learning is faster but rank advancement might be slower. Teaching only one version of a technique can make rank advancement faster, as students master the test arts, but may leave the students less versatile.

Feeling confused, one of my students left my dojo to join another, where she believed she could learn "just one way" to do each technique. She had the grace to visit me later, saying her new Japanese instructor showed a variation on a technique, grinned, and announced, "Silly to know only one way to do a technique!"

This suggests that we must individualize our teaching. I would have better served my departed student by saying, "Okay, just practice it this way," while allowing students of a different temperament to learn variations. Different students have different learning styles. Ideally, each style can be met by a different way of teaching.

Sometimes a student who is chronically clumsy — as I was in my early aikido years — can't seem to do the technique that was instructed, but accidentally does something resembling a different aikido technique. Best to tell that student, "Good! That wasn't the one I wanted you to do, but it's a good technique! Can you do it again? Class, let's everyone try the technique Steve invented!"

Our job as teachers is not to advance students quickly in rank, but to teach them aikido. We tell impatient students that rank without mastery is meaningless; it devalues the dojo and the art, and serves the student poorly.

As I noted in this book's introduction, my teaching emphasizes balance and body knowledge. I have to weigh this emphasis against a student's natural desire to have his or her progress recognized by rank promotion, and adjust my teaching accordingly.

42
What's Your Metaphor?

◄◦►

Visiting the Kiyomizu dera (清水寺) in Kyoto more than 40 years ago, it occurred to me that substituting 気 for 清 would yield the same pronunciation, *kiyomizu,* but imply "ki flow like water," an inspiring image of eddies and flows. After a 2019 class in Shanghai, one advanced student said to me, "Your aikido is like water." I'm pleased that that image has become reality, these decades later.

Despite that my Western birth-sign is Pisces, I am not attached to the water metaphor.

Now let's talk about you. At some stage of your practice, the idea of *fudoshin* (immovable mind) may capture your attention, and you'll spend some months cultivating fudoshin in your practice. The following year you may want to work on relaxation as you practice. Another year it may be "yielding," "connecting to the earth," "breathing," or "harmonizing."

No shame in this. F. Scott Fitzgerald (among others) wrote that consistency is the refuge of small minds. Feel free to be inconsistent in your conception of your practice, even as you are consistent in your practice. A metaphor, however useful, is just a metaphor. Even as you *apply* your metaphor-of-the-moment to your practice, do not *identify* the metaphor with the real, physical practice, and don't identify your self with the metaphor.

Different metaphors will best serve you at different stages of your progress, and keep you motivated as your enthusiasm for the previous metaphor has faded.

"What's the Soup of the Day?" a customer asked. The cook replied, "It's Cream of the Soup of Yesterday." Don't be like that chef; keep your metaphors fresh and new.

43
Sword and Staff

◄○►

In the 1970s, elder Japanese instructors would tell us what splendid fellows they had been during World War II — feeding Chinese orphans, only firing over the heads of opposing soldiers, etc. Take it or leave it, as you please. I believed less than half of it.

There's a reason for this odd chapter opening. I'll get to it in a moment.

It should be clear that feeling an uke's balance or lack of balance, so basic to learning aikido, just doesn't happen in kumitachi (unless uke flinches). Bokken suburi (cuts and thrusts) build upper-body strength — which we emphasize is irrelevant to aikido! — though learning to cut and thrust with good coordination is unarguably valuable.

As for self-defense, sword takeaways, which we practice as *bokken tori*, are far inferior to "sword runaways," that is, getting as far away from the swordsman as you can. The takeaways are only for instances in which you cannot run away. Estimate the probability (a number between zero and one) that you'll be attacked by a swordsman on the street. Multiply that by the probability that you'll be unable to run away. The result will be a very small number, close to zero. Use that number to decide how much time you will spend practicing bokken tori in class.

Some martial artists keep a sword by their bedside, intending to threaten nocturnal home invaders with it. Assuming you do not do this, the probability is likewise tiny that you will ever attack someone else with a sword. (If you do, Toyoda Shihan advised,

strike to the head. A body strike will slow you down, he said, as it's difficult to extract the sword from the victim's trunk, and a second hostile might be approaching. Memorable advice! But in all likelihood, advice you will never use.)

If you never in your life hold a sword, you can still become a perfectly adequate aikidoist.[6] Swordsmanship is part of aikido's heritage, and raising the arms and cutting *as if* with a sword is basic to a great many unarmed aikido movements. The key phrase "as if" raises the question of whether the sword is valuable for us as a physical sword, as a metaphor, or as a bit of history.

It's good to know history. Yet there is always someone who knows more history than you. There is no one, on the other hand, who can practice (or benefit from practicing) more than several hours per day. Therefore, practicing unarmed technique, on the mat and in your head, is a surer path to mastery than swinging a sword as a nod to aikido history — however respectful that nod might be.

The history that you read and hear might be biased, or even fake. (I cleverly motivated this argument in the chapter opening.) Your own practice is authentic! Practice sincerely, and rely on your practice.

The jo presents a somewhat different perspective. My good friend teaches aikido at a community college. His students tend to do poorly in their physics classes, defeated by the classical mechanics equations. He makes them learn the equations for levers (in physical education class!) as prerequisite for handling the jo. In contrast, I've taught aikido in a graduate technological institute.

---

[6] Some schools will vociferously hold the opposite view. I hope they will "agree to disagree," as a teacher in one such school has graciously done already. Of course I am not advising you against practicing sword.

My students were engineering postgrads. They knew the equations inside out, but put an actual stick in their hands and they were all fumble-fingers.

Your students' jo experience will likely be somewhere between those extremes.

In principle, jo nage and jo tori should be simple as pie. If you can't do an aikido technique *with all that leverage,* it seems unlikely you'll ever be able to do the technique at all. You can demonstrate the value of leverage by executing jo nage while loosely holding the jo only with the thumb and forefinger of each hand.

In fact now that I think of it, I'd like to experiment by having beginners start with jo nage before letting them try unarmed technique!

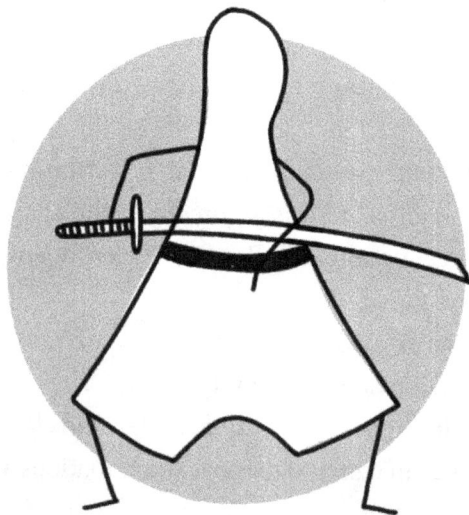

44

Teaching Aiki Sword

—◁○▷—

The earlier chapter "**Kumitachi Make No Sense**" explained why sword practice baffles students. Beginners are enchanted by holding a weapon for the first time, and by the mechanics of suburi. Soon, though, their confusion about the practice comes to the fore.

Fumio Toyoda would stop a shomen cut well before it reached horizontal. "Cut your opponent's head," he taught, "It's quicker than a body strike, easier to get your sword out again, and the guy is just as dead." Ueshiba O-Sensei preferred "navel to navel" strikes,[7] finishing with the hilt near your belly-button and the point near the opponent's. Why the difference? Toyoda taught suburi with self-defense (or rather, effective offense) in mind; O-Sensei sought spiritual unification with the opponent.

Other teachers stress the dialog of cut, parry, cut, parry, or emphasize angles and tai sabaki. Some present suburi as calisthenic misogi, as in the "thousand cuts on New Years Day" tradition. Still others teach what their teachers taught, without reflecting about the practice's purpose.

Each teaching is worthy. Each prescribes a different way of cutting. Each depends on a different underlying rationale. A cut that's wrong under one rationale is a perfect cut under another rationale. A cut that leaves an opening can be "wrong" under one rationale; under another, it might be deliberate bait, to lead uke to a vulnerable position. Confusing!

---

[7] https://www.aikidosangenkai.org/blog/an-interview-aikido-shihan-hiroshi-isoyama-part-1/

In your own dojo or when you visit another school, the sensei may yell, "That's wrong! Why are you doing that??" yet does not offer a reason why your cut might be wrong. Even worse, this sensei implies that it's wrong in an absolute sense, not just wrong for the particular teaching goal.

Understand why your teacher taught bokken the way he or she did. Recognize that your thoughtful students will become confused and resistant, unless you explain the rationale for your particular sword practice. Rather than chastise a "wrong" cut, explain *why* you want the student to cut in a different way.

WHY DO WE DO THIS? REFLECTIONS ON TRAINING FOR BOTH TEACHERS AND STUDENTS

45

Intention

-◁◦▷-

I can't recall exactly what Toyoda Sensei asked me to do, on that day 25 years ago. I do remember his request struck me as difficult to carry out, and perhaps not really necessary.

"I'll try," I waffled.

Sensei just looked at me.

"OK, I get it. There is no try, only do or don't do." I weakly attempted to mollify Sensei with this quote from *Star Wars'* Yoda.

"That's right," Sensei replied. "But there is also intention."

I've given thought to what he meant.

What is intention? Where does it come from? We can see "do." "Don't do" is pretty easy to notice too. We can't see intention. It would have been unlike Toyoda, a Zen master, to ask me to believe in something I could see, much less something invisible. If I were to say, "I decided," or "I intend," Sensei would have demanded to know who intended. Intention might, then, have something to do with ego.

Since intention also seems connected to making a decision, and I have published a book on Zen and decision making, my students tease me: "Sensei, did you figure out what intention is yet? Going to write a sequel?" A proper Zen master would say intention pops spontaneously from the enlightened mind, like water from a spring. This is trite, though, and not too informative.

(In martial art, we speak of reading the attacker's intention. However, we also say that the moment of attack is a moment of

insanity on the attacker's part. We would prefer to know the nature and origin of intention in the sane mind.)

The Western psychological literature on the subject is murky too. In the '70s, Julian Jaynes suggested that Homeric times brought a shift in human consciousness. The *Odyssey* reflects a world in which the voices in a man's head were presumed to be the gods sending directions. Characters in the later *Iliad* understand internal voices to be their own, talking to themselves. (Not much improvement, if you ask me.)

Later research seemed to show that the cerebral cortex censors impulses to speech or action, but does not originate them. Experiments that allowed subjects to self-report the moment of decision revealed that nerve signals to (for example) a finger were on their way well before the reported instant of deciding to move the finger. Whether the original impulse came from the old limbic ("lizard") portion of the subject's brain or from some telepathic connection with the Great Mind of the Universe was never settled. Either way, though the cortical censor can sometimes abort an action that comes from elsewhere, the censor and the illusion of making the decision in the cortex are sideshows to the main event.

Actually, this sounds very Zen, but isn't a really satisfying answer to the question. And why my lizard brain, or yours, would decide to prove the Pythagorean theorem or read *War and Peace*... well, let's not go there.

In 1992, D.C. Dennett mustered powerful arguments against the notion of the "Cartesian theater." The Cartesian theater is the assumption — implicit in ordinary conversation and in much research, too — that there is a central control center, something like a little person sitting in a tiny director's chair in front of a screen in your head. The Mini-Me sorts sense impressions, forms intentions, makes decisions, and sends out action orders.

The problems with the Cartesian theater are obvious. (What's inside the little guy's head?) It's just that it's hard to imagine an alternative that works. Robert A. Heinlein drew a deliciously ironic map of the Cartesian theater, and then in one last sentence demolished it:

> What was an ego? He didn't know, but he knew he was one. By which he did not mean his body, nor, by damn, his genes. He could localize it — on the centerline, forward of his ears, back of his eyes, and about four centimeters down from the top of the skull — no, more like six. That was where he *himself* lived — when he was home — he would bet on it, to the nearest centimeter. He *knew* closer than that, but he couldn't get in and measure it. Of course, he wasn't home all the time.[8]

Heinlein wrote this in 1942. Fifty years later, science caught up with literature when Dennett authoritatively dispensed with the Cartesian theater. With what did he replace it? Echoing the Homeric Greeks, Dennett sketched a brain made up of semi-autonomous personae. His modern twist is that these personae are organic computers, parallel processing at such a level of complexity that self-consciousness emerges as an epiphenomenon (Translation: sideshow to the main event). Intention may originate in any one of these parallel processors — or in several at once, with some accidental algorithm allowing one or another to dominate.

How does this help us make the decision to make the intention to make a commitment to a teacher? Well, it doesn't.

And that suggests we might try to reframe the question's context. Seeing the question of intention as coming from Fumio Toyoda the

---

[8] Robert A. Heinlein, *Beyond This Horizon*. Signet, New York © 1942, p. 127.

Zen master led to all the fruitless twists and turns above. However, the question as asked by F. Toyoda, the man from Japan, is more straightforward. A person steeped in the samurai tradition — as distinct from the Zen tradition — values sincerity (*makoto*) and obligation (*giri*). In this framework, proper behavior consists of "making up your mind, saying what you're gonna do, and doing what you said you were gonna," and shouldering the consequences if you don't. In other words, it's about correct social behavior, not about deep psychology.

There are, nonetheless, a couple of Zen lessons here. First, Western science has come to an Eastern-sounding conclusion about the brain: "There's nobody home." The notion can leave Westerners feeling adrift without a lifeboat. Zen students, though, have had lots of practice in dealing with this reality, and the progress of Western psychology is just a further validation of Zen practice, if such is needed.[9]

Second, beware of getting stuck to assumptions! My implicit assumption that my Sensei was imparting a Zen lesson stalled my understanding of "intention" for many years. Yes, a Zen master always speaks as a Zen master. But not everything he says is a koan. When the master says, "I'm hungry," sometimes it just means it's time for lunch.

---

[9] Around 2017, long after I first drafted this essay, a number of books appeared with titles like Where Buddhism Meets Neuroscience, and Beyond the Self: Conversations Between Buddhism and Neuroscience.

46
Duality: The Power of Two

◄○►

"Jeanne, we're all practicing. Why aren't you on the mat?"

Jeanne, who was pinching her nose with a handkerchief, answered, "I hab a nodebleed, Dzentsei."

Jeanne had been spending her daytime hours starting a new company. Her worry about the company had distracted her during practice, and she had left her nose in the path of her partner's atemi. Always intellectually interested in how her martial art practice could help her be a better entrepreneur, Jeanne thought wryly that she had just learned a painful lesson in that subject: When entering the dojo, leave business worries at the door.

"Come here, Jeanne, and don't get blood on the mat." Herring Sensei clapped his hands twice, a signal for the students to stop practicing.

He directed Jeanne to sit on the mat in seiza posture. "How do you cure a nosebleed?" he asked the students, who had circled closely to show their concern for Jeanne.

"Direct pressure," said one.

"Ice," offered another.

"Lying down."

"Drinking water out of the wrong side of the glass."

"Here's a reliable method," Sensei said. "It may scare you, but it won't hurt." He held Jeanne's forehead with his left hand. With the blade of his right hand, he lightly but sharply hit the back of her neck — two rapid strikes in quick succession — while shouting kiai. His shattering cry, "Hiiyaaaa!" startled everyone.

"You can take away the cloth now," he said.

Jeanne removed the kerchief from her nose. After a moment, she and another student who was peering up Jeanne's nostrils simultaneously announced, "It stopped!"

"Sensei, does that always work?" asked a young man on the edge of the crowd.

"It won't stanch a gunshot wound," noted Herring, who was always amused by students' reaction to this demonstration, "but your ordinary, garden-variety nosebleed, yes, nearly a hundred percent of the time."

"Why does it work?" the same man asked.

"When I was a student in Japan in the 70s," Sensei began, and the students groaned aloud. With Herring Sensei, they knew, shaggy-dog stories were more common than straight answers. They settled to comfortable positions on the practice mat, hoping their teacher would in due course get to the point.

"As I say, even into the 1970s, scholars were debating whether the atomic bomb should have been dropped on Nagasaki. You know, don't you, that the first bomb fell on Hiroshima, and about a week later, after the Nagasaki bombing, Japan surrendered, ending World War II. The atom bomb was a new weapon with horrific destructive ability, and subjected its survivors to unknown radiation effects. Why, the scholars asked, was it necessary to drop the second bomb? What do you think? Jeanne?"

"Was it revenge for Japanese war atrocities?" Jeanne ventured.

Another student guessed aloud, "Maybe when the military has a new weapon they just like to use it."

Their teacher replied, "Maybe those two things factored in. But the consensus of scholars and strategists is that it was a careful, sober, and perhaps reluctant decision on the part of the U.S. War Department. First, they considered the alternative. If the bomb did not make Japan surrender, Americans would have had

to invade the Japanese homeland. Millions of people might have died in combat and bombing — far more than the body count from the Hiroshima and Nagasaki bombs — including huge numbers of American casualties."

"But maybe one atomic bomb would have prevented that," noted a student.

"Exactly! There was another reason for the decision," Sensei said. "The second reason embodied a very profound principle of strategy and tactics. Do you know that the number 'two' doesn't exist?"

"I believe it's between one and three," a student helpfully interjected.

"Sure, as an abstraction. But scientists believe there may be unique objects or events in the universe — things there are only one of, like perhaps a one-of-a-kind black hole — and there are lots of things that there are three or more of, like stars. But they have not ever identified a natural object or event that there is only two of. Did I get that grammar right?"

The same student, now less skeptical and more intrigued, asked, "What about positive and negative electrical charges? That's only two kinds of charge."

"Good question, but again, positive and negative are principles, not natural objects or events. Besides, it depends how you count. Did you hear about the neutron who ordered a beer in a bar? When he asked for the tab, the bartender said..."

"... For you, no charge!" the class chorused in unison.

"Seriously, you might say yin and yang are two principles, but they are only meaningful when you consider their interaction — which is a third thing. Two implies three.

"So what is the strategic power of the non-existent number two? I'm talking about human interactions now, not astronomy."

Jeanne spoke up. "You gave us a clue when you said 'natural object or event.' If you see just two of something, it means it's artificial. Or that there's intention involved."

"Bingo! And what did that imply for the end of the Second World War?"

"One atomic explosion might have been... an accident." Jeanne was thinking even as she spoke. "Even, perhaps, a natural disaster that the Americans foresaw — and not a weapon at all! Not a reason to stop fighting. Two explosions — wait, make that two explosions and *only* two explosions — had to have been man-made. The Japanese would know that it was an artificially created event, and they'd know that it was a reliable weapon..."

"Just the Japanese?" Herring asked.

"Oh, no," the young man who had spoken earlier sighed as he realized the sad truth, "It reassured the Americans too." He brightened up. "And alerted the Russians... and told the Japanese the U.S. was willing to stop..."

"In any event," Herring said, "the signal was sent and received. It cost a tragic number of lives to send that signal, but it saved many more lives, and years of strife. Now, why am I telling you this, Jeanne?"

"Not to help me end World War II, I guess," Jeanne smiled. "Other people took care of that a long time ago. Ah! Got it! You're telling me not to take my company public yet, not until our second product is launched and selling. One product might be a fluke as far as Wall Street is concerned; two products mean we're a real, reliable, promising company. Two products, and our investment bank can float us at a much higher valuation!"

"Yes, Jon?" Sensei recognized a student who was waving an arm.

"I'm a quality engineer at a tools company," said Jon, "and I've been wondering whether manufacturing a product to a tolerance of

ten decimal places and six sigmas is really quality. I mean, if it makes no difference in performance that a customer cares about, it's just quantity, not quality. So, how do we know if a customer cares? Not from total product sales; a customer might buy the item once just to try it, or to follow an industry fad. But if he buys it twice, it means he really likes it. So I've come to believe that repeat-buying is the only true measure of product quality, and that's another instance of your power of two."

"And any time you can do exactly the same thing twice, with a customer or a competitor, they know it wasn't just dumb luck, they can believe you are reliable," another student added. "And Jon's girlfriend has been trying to get Jon to say he loves her. If you mean it, Jon, it looks like you'd better tell her twice!"

Jon, embarrassed, redirected the discussion. "I see why it's a powerful signal in almost any kind of strategic or tactical situation, in business and in politics too," he said.

"Yes… and no," Herring twinkled.

"What do you mean 'no,' Sensei? I think that's the right answer."

"What you said is correct," Sensei replied, "but I asked Jeanne why I was telling her about the power of two. I was saying all this to make a point about nosebleeds!" The class laughed.

"Your body has evolved a 'fight or flight' mechanism. When you are threatened, your heart accelerates, your senses sharpen, and the capillaries near the surface of your body constrict, to stem blood loss in case you are cut or bitten."

"Bitten, Sensei?"

"Yeah, by a saber-tooth tiger or something, I suppose. If you can make your capillaries constrict, your nose stops bleeding. But the body has to know the attack is real — not, for example, just a falling twig."

"That's why you hit me twice," Jeanne said.

"That's right. To stop the bleeding, shout loudly and hit twice. Not too hard, this is your friend's neck, after all. Both strikes must be within a space of less than half a second. This convinces your friend's system that it has experienced 'two of the same thing.' Never fails.[10]

"Let's not end this conversation without noting that the U.S. and Japan have been friends and allies for seventy years. This, Jeanne, is because the relationship has usually been well-managed. Yin and yang, and their interaction. To the beginner, one and one makes two. To a more sophisticated student, one and one makes three. To the realized individual, the realized manager, one and one makes…"

"Transcendence," Jeanne said quietly.

"Bingo," said Herring, "and how do you transcend dualism? Practice! Everyone back on the mat!"

---

[10] Koichi Tohei taught me the nosebleed cure. He used it dozens of times with never a failure, and so have I.

47

When Times Get Tough, the Tough Stay Centered: The Way of Peace

—◇—

There are two kinds of people in the world: Those who divide people into two kinds, and those who don't. Or anyway, certain kinds of people say so!

Though the wars in Iraq are officially over, Americans and Iraqis still die violently there almost every day. The 9/11 Trade Center attacks are still being investigated. In addition to their other causes — revenge, oil, the arms trade — these tragedies happened because of beliefs. In this chapter I wish to write about our relations, as aikidoists, with people who hold different beliefs.

An obvious way to divide people into two kinds is to distinguish young people from old people. The young naturally believe that all people are the same under the skin, and that all differences are petty ones, easily overcome. The old consider this view dangerously naïve. Both are correct. We shall see that as Zen martial artists, we can accept this seeming paradox and emerge from it with the right action.

Let's try some other ways of sorting people into types. "Alphas" (as we will call them) grow older but continue to embrace the youthful notion that 'we can all get along.' They are remarkably willing to concede the validity of diverse views. We may suspect that Alphas have not had their uncritical tolerance tested very severely — for example, in wartime or through losing a loved one in the World Trade towers on 9/11 — and we suspect further that

they are wishy-washy about their own core values. We might feel protective or even envious of Alphas. We might hope they do not become disillusioned, even though they're avoiding some hard questions. (Once they stop avoiding, reformed Alphas can become good aikido students.)

More usually, people — we'll call this kind "Betas" — believe their own values or religion are correct and others are simply wrong. However, courtesy and hospitality are among Betas' common values, and they are able to forge a civil society together with non-co-religionists. The uneasy balance between their prejudices and their better natures never tips them into violence in daily life. However, politicians may be able to persuade Betas that organized violence is justified.

"Gammas" feel comfortable in their parochial traditions, and stick to them. They know, however, that most of their traditional practices are, in a pinch, dispensable. They can easily distinguish their dispensable practices from their non-negotiable core values. The core values often include the Golden Rule, respect for human life, and helping the needy. These fine people are pleased, though not surprised, to find that neighbors from very different ethnic backgrounds and religious traditions have the same irreplaceable core values. It takes an extraordinary person to rely on an irreducible core of faith, rather than on outward religious trappings, and Gammas are almost always a minority in their own communities.

Still another kind of people, "Deltas," believes their religion is right, that others are unfortunately misinformed, and that missionary work is therefore in order. Deltas are annoying, but as long as they are not violently coercive, persistently courteous resistance usually leads to peaceable coexistence with them — or mutual avoidance.

So far, we're doing pretty well. Alphas, Betas, Gammas, Deltas: Different beliefs, and differing attitudes about different beliefs, and as long as the Betas are calm, no blows have been struck. (This is easy to say, perhaps, for a Zen martial artist who has no beliefs. But we respect the role of belief in other people's lives. The Zen scholar D.T. Suzuki, after expounding at great length on the reasons prayer is absolutely useless, sheepishly concluded, "But we all do it anyway.") So we are okay with people who have almost any kind of belief, approach, or attitude.

Almost. Because there are those who are violently coercive about their beliefs, or just violent. These "Epsilons" think people who don't share their beliefs and practices are evil, and must be eliminated, enslaved, or forcibly converted. In dealing with Epsilons, job number one for the aikidoist is keep your center; don't become like them. On the mat, you do not punch people who punch you; you respond using your techniques, not theirs. Off the mat, the same: Do not respond in kind to negative incoming energy. Respond using what you've learned and who you are. That is your strength.

Job number two, don't provoke them. You have no ego, nothing to prove. In fact, though you do not respect Epsilons' violent proclivities, you do recognize the forces that nurtured their extremism. Epsilons in the Middle East are hurting from repression in their own societies, a feeling of being disrespected internationally, and the drowning of the finer sides of their culture under Euro-Disney and golden arches.

There are also Epsilons in American society, and Betas who actively or passively abet their violence. We're not in a simple good-guys-here-bad-guys-there situation. "If only there were evil people somewhere insidiously committing evil deeds and it were necessary only to separate them from the rest of us and destroy them,"

Aleksandr Solzhenitsyn wrote. "But the line dividing good and evil cuts through the heart of every human being. And who is willing to destroy a piece of his own heart?"

By recognizing destructive forces and extremism we do not validate them. We are not Alphas. When we harmonize with attackers, we feel no separation from them. They are another side of ourselves, but a side we don't like. We work on them by working on ourselves, through our practice, through the way we treat other people, and through the clarity of what we say and do. Keeping one-point is not passive; we may initiate bold projects to set modern cultural forces in more constructive directions. Our projects may involve outreach to Gammas living in societies on the "other side" of the conflict. In any case, our initiatives show the clarity that comes from no-self.

Unfortunately, this is not an answer that will bring peace to the world. It will not, in all likelihood, prevent further terrorist attacks. It is, though, what will bring peace to you and me: Keeping our centers, staying true to ourselves and our teachers, and being true to our practice of aikido.

48

Victims at Work

◄○►

Our university hired Janet, an attorney, to brief the faculty on workplace harassment issues.

She wisely confined herself to explaining the law. She did not venture into discussions of respect, self-esteem, or customs — gray areas in which organizations cannot, in any event, legislate. Nevertheless, Janet's talk painted a picture of a university peopled by perpetrators and victims.

The dramatis personae in the world of workplace harassment are: Rights groups, national legislators, employing firms, employing firms' lawyers, employees, and courts. Small wonder that all discussion is framed in terms of perps and vics.

A classic police victim profile study, however, gives us a different view. In this study, convicted muggers were shown films of different actors walking down the street. The convicts were asked, "Which of these people would you attack if you were out there?" Overwhelmingly, pedestrians shuffling along, looking at the pavement, shoulders hunched, were identified by the convicts as prime targets. Other filmed actors strode along confidently, arms and legs swinging freely, with an upright posture and forward gaze. The muggers did not tag the latter actors as potential victims.

Why don't we teach "how not to be a victim"? U.S. law requires companies to post notices of the acts that constitute harassment, but does not require employers to train employees in how to avoid becoming victims.

Indeed, the law takes pains not to do the latter, for fear that a "blame the victim" mentality might re-assert itself ("She dressed provocatively and invited the advance"). However, if you are lucky to have a good martial art instructor demonstrate to your class, you will see that: (i) Posture, confidence, and gait can be taught and learned; and (ii) By learning escape and control techniques, you can reduce your fear of being grabbed in an office hallway or garage.

Confident adults understand what even kids know: "Sticks and stones may break my bones, but words, they cannot hurt me." Moreover, popular business writers have repeatedly shown how being a victim is detrimental to business success.

A company or university wants to be productive. What ultimately limits productivity? A firm full of safe employees who maintain a victim mentality, or a firm full of employees who have taken control of their lives?

How much better it would be to teach employees not to be victims!

49
Why Do Bad Things Happen to Good People?

—◄o►—

Perhaps you started your study of aikido because you wanted more power, more control, over yourself and your life. Maybe you even wanted power over other people, or at least the ability to defend yourself. As earlier chapters have emphasized, physical skills and situational awareness increase your chances of staying safe, but there are no guarantees.

Like other practitioners, you are drawn to aikido because it reinforces your better instincts. You see yourself as a "good person," and want to see the good in others. Your practice of aikido, the art of compassion, may lead you to ponder the question, why do bad things happen to good people?

This universal and terrible question does have an answer. The answer is less satisfying than we might wish, because we cannot change the fact that bad things will sometimes happen to good people. Yet the answer is helpful because it is simple and it gives us a way to cope with the horror of America's recent tragedies — terrorist acts, epidemics, school shootings, and loss of our young in wars.

There are three kinds of bad things. First, one person may intentionally harm another. Second, a person may be harmed while intentionally taking a risk, for example, by mountain-climbing. And third — classically caricatured by a piano falling from an upper window onto a passerby — nature may, without intention, do a job on an unsuspecting innocent.

Each of these bad things makes us unhappy.

The key to understanding the first two is the idea of free will. To make this clear, consider three imaginary worlds, each having different rules about free will:

➤ In the first world, there is no free will. A person in a world without free will can hardly be happier than even the unhappiest free person — notwithstanding that bad things happen to free people. Being a puppet on a string is no fun.

➤ In the second world, only one person has free will. The one free person in this world can find no satisfaction in a world of puppets — even if he is the puppet master. He will experience no surprises, no personal growth, and ultimate boredom.

➤ In the third world, everyone has free will *except one person.* This person fears his powerlessness. He hates his inability to do anything to help himself or others. (Fear and hate may not be possible without free will. But this is our thought experiment, so we can make the rules.)

The third imaginary world can sound very much like our own everyday world, especially when we are battered by attackers we cannot see or find. We may wish to become more powerful than our attackers. However, no matter how strong a person is, there is always someone who is stronger. No matter how rich he is, somewhere someone is richer. A rare person may become the strongest or richest, but only for a short time. In other words, some kinds of powerlessness are inevitable, and fearing powerlessness is a waste of time. Our security lies in what is in our hearts, not in what is in our muscles or wallets. A better use of our free will is to choose how we will think, and how we will treat our families, friends and neighbors.

The "imaginary worlds" exercise shows that if one person has free will, then everyone else should too. Not only is that fair, but it is what thinking people really want. Unfortunately, to enjoy free will is to accept that some people may decide to harm other people. There is no need for a discussion of the nature of evil; free will means freedom to decide between a right action and a wrong action.

It also means freedom to decide to climb the Himalayas, investigate the Bermuda Triangle, or enlist in the military in wartime. Free will would meaningless if we did not also have the ability to know (or estimate) the likely consequences of our actions. For many and varied reasons — to save another life, to find new resources, to feel more alive, or just to explore — people willingly embrace significant probabilities of injury or death. This is their freedom.

These adventurous folks would probably argue that people who stay at home in bed risk a great deal, too. Stay-at-homes risk the loss of their physical health and their social lives. They risk missing opportunities to take on responsibilities, and to experience the variety of the world they were born into.

This leaves the third question: What about the hurricane, the earthquake, the falling anvil that wipes out ordinary, intelligent, loving, risk-averse people who have plans and hopes for their future? Applying cold logic to this emotionally charged question may be an unattractive thing to do, but the fact is that the question invites circular reasoning. Life is fragile, and for that reason we consider life to be precious. So far, so good. Then we muse, "Life is so precious, what a tragedy that it is as delicate and vulnerable as it is."

We also manage to make life's fragility a desirable state of affairs. We are attracted to a potential spouse or lover in part because of his or her vulnerability. We enjoy actors and comics who can reveal the vulnerable everyman in their characters. We have myths and

stories featuring immortals who wish most of all to become mortal. Cinematic examples are *City of Angels*, starring Meg Ryan and Nicholas Cage, and *Highlander*, with Christopher Lambert and Sean Connery.

Is this why an anvil falling on a cartoon character is funny? We call this kind of humor "absurd." It tells us we face risks that we don't know about, in addition to the ones we are aware of, that we worry too much about low-probability events, that anything can happen, and that our lives are indeed fragile and in many ways uncontrollable. Sometimes we laugh at absurd humor out of nervous discomfort. Sometimes we laugh with joy, realizing there is nothing we can do about it, so let's get on with living.

Sensible precautions against terrorism? Yes. Trying to be more aware of our surroundings? Of course! But we are not going to forbid pianos and anvils to upper-story tenants. Denying the upstairs neighbors their free will won't make us any happier.

However, our martial art training pushes our awareness "out of our heads" and into the enhanced perception of our surroundings that we call "presence of mind." This makes it more likely (but no guarantees!) that you'll duck just in time, or push that elderly fellow out of the path of the careening bus.

50
Aikido and Beyond

—◦—

Should we take aikido beyond the traditional forms? Take aikido beyond what Ueshiba O-Sensei taught? I am cautiously in favor of it, though with all kinds of caveats.

This is a controversy as old as aikido itself. O-Sensei followed Shinto and infused aikido training with Shinto ritual. Koichi Tohei Sensei, whom O-Sensei named as his successor, was Buddhist, and didn't conduct classes the same way O-Sensei did. This caused a major schism in aikido in the early 1970s, about the time I started training.

O-Sensei presented aikido as a universal art. My late teacher Fumio Toyoda believed aikido was inseparable from Japanese culture. Who was right? And if Toyoda Sensei was right, then what Japanese culture was he talking about? Shinto? Buddhist?

Tohei Sensei instituted "ki classes" for people unable to practice aikido. I teach ki principles for tango, and I teach intro to martial art for yoga practitioners. I have to ask myself, did Tohei Sensei send his Japanese students to *misogi* training so they'd be better aikidoists, or so they'd be better people? Did he do it to mold the students into the people he wanted them to be, or into the people *they* wanted to be? After my best struggle with those questions, which cannot be answered definitively now that the principals are dead, I teach what I teach. If people keep coming, I keep teaching. If nobody comes, I stop. Gotta let these things go without too much disappointment, but of course with some analysis.

So, how much to go beyond the traditional seems to depend on context — cultural context and you might say demographic context. Many teachers have taken aikido in different directions. I'm comfortable with some of them, not comfortable with others.

Here's the thing: Ki principles can be taught without ever mentioning aikido. So, there's no danger of corrupting aikido! My own book on Zen for managers and decision makers had just one chapter that was explicitly about aikido. A Zen monk challenged the book, but I convinced him it did not unduly bend Zen out of shape. We have to tread carefully when we put new interpretations on venerable wisdom.

Toyoda Sensei said, never forget that aikido is martial art. In a *dan* examination at a Toyoda dojo, if you're asked, "What is aikido?" your first response better be "Aikido is a martial art." After that, you're free to further define aikido in whatever way you want. Toyoda and the fellow students were sincerely interested in each candidate's take on What is Aikido, but the core description had to be there.

When we say it's martial art, that means we must face life and death squarely, training and training in order to skillfully maintain life and liberty in any situation. Conquer death, even though we know we're going to die anyway. When we remember this, it's harder to segue into seemingly related but quite insipid ideas like pacifism, one-day mindfulness seminars, or niceness — the kinds of things often referred to as Buddhism Lite.

I don't think this is the view of a rigid traditionalist or the view of an aggressive personality (as some of my readers must be suspecting at this moment). I have spent more than 45 years believing in and trying to live O-Sensei's ideal that aikido is the way of compassion. And yes, aikido is indeed the martial art that avoids unnecessary damage to an attacker. These qualifications don't change the

fact that we cannot leave behind the core, that is, that aikido is martial art.

Once we agree to maintain that core, I guess we can take aikido in new directions. Like Tohei Sensei, we might want to do that in a way that serves people who are unable, either physically or temperamentally, to practice aikido. Or maybe as a teaser, to entice people to aikido, by meeting them halfway to their own terrain. But never by diluting the core of aikido.

I teach ki principles for tangueros and tangueras, and I teach conflict management to business people, using ki principles. We can find the natural bridges between our territory and theirs: Attentiveness to a partner's balance, in aikido and in tango; and for yoga people the legendary roots of east Asian martial art in the Indian yogi Bodhidharma who traveled to China's Shaolin temples, adapting yoga movements for the monks' self-defense.

Maybe you could teach elderly people how to fall down safely. An aunt of mine broke both wrists in a fall. Geez, Auntie, I said, you should try to fall on your tuchis, it has more padding than your wrists. My father, then 91, unwisely broke a fall with... his nose! And broke his nose, of course. I'd guess most of us envision "aikido extensions" in terms of expanding consciousness or spirituality. I'm all for that. But if you want to quickly create a big social benefit with your aikido extensions, teach old people how to fall down!

I've bridged East and West with a classroom strategy game called Quest for the Sword. In this game, students seek Katsu-jinken, the Sword that Protects Life. The game requires players to research aikido-related ideas like fudoshin, sen no sen, and zan-shin. The game over-intellectualizes things that should be learned in a more experiential way, but hey, I am a professor and that's what we do at universities.

The game distinguishes three Japanese cultures: the samurai culture, the company or *kaisha* culture, and Buddhist culture. The three have some values that overlap, and some that are distinct. Obviously people from all three cultures practice aikido. So, we might ask Mr. Toyoda if he were here, "Just what Japanese culture are you talking about?"

It's ironic that O-Sensei himself taught aikido in two different ways, one style in Wakamatsu-cho and another in Iwama. Some of you are aware of the historical reasons for that. You might also wonder why we place so much emphasis on wrist-grabbing attacks. Does it strike you as unrealistic? It stems from movements meant to prevent an opponent from drawing his sword. We don't, these days, live in a society of sword-carriers. So a change in emphasis might be justified. There is room for eclecticism in our interpretations of aikido.

But be careful. Tohei Sensei was careful. His ki class students could see dramatic mind-body effects immediately. He knew that if you teach something without a visible manifestation, you risk being tagged as a charlatan. The other day a blogger was touting a "neuroscience advance" that could produce in a few hours the same brain state as ten years of meditation. He claimed he isn't making money on it, but just wants to bring the benefit to more people. If you try too hard to proselytize — especially, as he is, a product with invisible benefits that's probably just another ineffective shortcut around long years of practice — you risk being seen as an insecure person who seeks validation by persuading others to adopt your view.

Visible manifestations can go wrong, too. One student showed up for practice wearing a beautifully made hakama patterned in the manner of his home country. It was quite appealing, a neat idea. Toyoda banished him from the mat. Tradition demands that we don't distract our fellow students from their practice. This is why

we stick to white or ivory *dogi*, black or blue *hakama*. So, starting an aikido fashion business is probably not a good idea. (Dojo t-shirts excepted, of course.)

There's an interesting new dance form called contact improvisation. You can see it on YouTube; it vaguely resembles aikido. It's all fine if practitioners say contact improv was inspired by aikido movements, which it was. There is no other connection with aikido, as it is not martial art. It would be ridiculous and insulting to aikidoists to claim otherwise.

Yet there comes a point at which every aikidoist must make aikido his own, or to put it another way, make her own aikido. You might remember Bruce Lee chiding a good technician that his martial art had no passion, no personality. Right on. After 1st dan or so, it's not good just to be parroting other people's movements. You need to show your examiners that you have internalized the art, made it your own, infused it with your own personality.

You cannot do that, though, until you have achieved near-mastery of *kihon waza,* basic technique. And by the time you've gained that mastery, the tradition is very much a part of your life. You respect it too much to go off on some tangent and still call it aikido. The flip side of that truth is that people who are on odd tangents, and calling it aikido, probably do not have expertise in aikido.

If you create your aikido extensions with very deep respect for the original tradition, and use language carefully, you'll be okay.

51
Women in Aikido

◄○►

Aikido is for everyone. Discriminating against a student on the basis of ethnicity, gender, religion, or disability is not allowable.

Students of all colors and ages practice together. Differently abled aikido students have found, with their senseis' help, creative ways to learn and execute aikido techniques, each tailored to the individual student's abilities.

Exclusion from the dojo should never stem from who you are, but only from how you act. Excessive aggression is the most common "bad act." Others would be acts that deliberately distract fellow students from their practice. (As I've mentioned, my teacher once ejected from the mat a student who showed up in a leopard-spot patterned hakama. He was allowed to return upon changing to standard uniform. Sensei complimented him on his creativity, but lectured him on its unfortunate impact.)

Yet, stuff happens. A beginner feels discomfort, entering a dojo where no one looks like her. Native students may act like they have to prove to a foreign visitor that they are tough martial artists. So, we must think about a topic — bigotry in aikido — that should be unthinkable.

As a general rule, dojos should be unsegregated, and biased only against chronic bad actors. It's the teacher's duty to maintain this rule, with just a few exceptions. Children's classes are an obvious exception.

Women's classes are a possible exception too. However, the decision to offer women-only classes is fraught with sensitive issues having to do with the woman's comfort level, the possibility of sexual misconduct among mixed students, and the environment that best encourages learning and continuation in aikido. On top of all this, the decision must sincerely avoid any hint of condescension toward female (or any other) students.

If aikido history doesn't adequately reveal the great achievements of female aikidoists, the performance of today's woman teachers and students surely does.

Women may come to the dojo with a history of experiences with overbearing or even abusive men. Naturally they will be skittish about practicing with or taking instruction from a man. I invite comments from women aikidoists who may have far deeper understanding of this than I do.

What I do understand thoroughly is that beginners muscle their way through techniques. As men are generally more muscular than women in the upper body, a man-woman beginner pairing can cause the woman to feel, erroneously, less capable than her partner. Retaining a woman student then depends on her coming to see that aikido is not done with the upper body, and that her leg is stronger than my arm. It's so nice to see the light bulb over her head as she realizes "Oh! This is why women are good at aikido!" I'm happy to say this has happened many times at my dojos.

Both of the problems in the last two paragraphs can be eased by, for example, an all-woman dojo or all-woman class, taught by a woman, until the student feels confident enough to do what's really necessary, which is to practice in a mixed class, with teacher and student working together to resolve or eliminate any classmate-inflicted indignities. This means dojo-cho of all-woman schools should expect, and indeed hope, to lose students as they reach this level.

Later, as confident and fully realized blackbelt aikidoists, women and men alike will simply shrug off any interpersonal insults, from outsiders or from unenlightened dojo classmates.

Recently a group of women aikidoists petitioned one of the prominent aikido federations to place more women as officials of the organization. Organizational indignities, like those addressed in the petition, quite likely bubble upward from ill-treatment of women in individual dojos, though this ill-treatment might be so low-key that instructors don't see it and students don't complain about it.

(The problem may also partially lie in cultural/communication gaps between non-Japanese students and senior Japanese teachers.)

I've emphasized the responsibility of aikido teachers. Yet it is the federations that accredit teachers. I would like to see these organizations require demonstrations of equity/inclusion competence for advancement in the teaching titles (e.g., fukushidoin, shidoin, sensei, shihan).

52
More Q&A: War and Peace

◄o►

Q. Why does war exist, and is war always bad? Do we fight because it is the right thing to do, like self-defense/prevention of harm? Or do we fight because we want something out of it, like getting enjoyment from anger and jealousy? If you had the chance to kill a ruthless dictator that could care less about peace, and you could kill him with one good sniper shot and get a clean getaway and no one knew that you did it, would you do it? Also, I grow suspicious of people who want peace and then create conflict, not peace, from their actions. -J

A. *J, we're going to dispense with goods and bads, and deal with "ises." Humans evolved, and evolution doesn't cut us much slack. If we were constituted differently, we might not have evolved and survived as a species. So men complaining about war may be like women complaining that men only think about sex: If either thing were different, we might not be here.*

The two, not surprisingly, are related. Bonobos, critters that look like chimpanzees, don't have war. They defuse conflicts by grooming each other and having sex. There aren't many bonobos left — despite all that sex. Chimps solve conflict by fighting. Then the winners have sex, that being the "something they get out of it." One strategy is better for procreation, the other better for protection, and a population needs both procreation and protection. There aren't many chimps left, either, but that's because of human-caused loss of chimp habitat, and there are (I think) more chimps than bonobos.

Is the same true for humans? A news article in 2003 noted that fully 12% of the current human population are direct descendants of Genghis Khan and his siblings. So historically, young men were motivated to go to war if it represented their only chance to "marry." Old men preferred to die in "glorious" battle because it beat the alternative, which involved having other people chew their food for them. That is to say, old age was not a pleasant affair before modern medicine, and some preferred to avoid it.

Today, some youngsters join the armed forces, even when war looms, because it's the only route out of a bad neighborhood and a life of poverty. (Actually not the only route: Selling drugs gets you out of poverty, affords the same probability of dying young, and you don't have to take orders from no stinkin' sergeants.) Others are duped into enlisting, believing their elders' bullshit about glory and justice.

Suppose we could only stop a genocide by going to war. All other things being equal, most people would like to see fewer deaths rather than more. All other things, though, are almost never equal, and I would tend to suspect decisions based on body-count arithmetic. In any case, each person must choose his own battles. We have a volunteer army, but they don't get to vote on where they will fight and where they won't. It might be worth letting them do that! Phil Ochs sang, "It's always the old who lead us to the war, always the young who fall." So it's like abortion, which is similarly tragic: I don't like abortion and I don't like war, but I'm not going to tell women — or men — what they may or may not do with their bodies.

I was raised to see preventing further genocides as a duty, and as a young man I was crushed to see the U.S. fail to act on that principle, for instance in Cambodia or Rwanda. (If you're a movie fan, watch The Killing Fields.*) Should future such situations arise,*

*I might well decide to rally others to a rescue mission, knowing vio-
lence might result but dedicating myself to minimizing it.*

*In wars of old, non-combatants suffered in serious, but indirect,
ways: via famine, rape, pillage. In today's wars, innocent bystand-
ers are far more likely than before to be killed directly. This can
happen in myriad ways, from mined rice fields to mis-aimed mis-
siles to crossfires in urban warfare. I hope young people desiring to
go to war will consider the near-inevitability of killing civilians, and
think twice and perhaps decide to stay home in Peoria.*

*In class, you mentioned Pearl Harbor, which was a famous fail-
ure of U.S. intelligence. I'll go so far as to say all war is a failure
of intelligence, planning, strategy, communication, or preparation.
If a threat is developing against you, you should, just as in aikido,
assemble overwhelming force at your opponent's weakest point.
You tell your opponent what you're going to do should he not stand
down, and then do it. This is how a mission should be defined and
executed. Sun Tzu said that, a long time ago.*

*Even military commanders who have mastered intelligence,
planning, strategy, communication and preparation get caught by
ego. They escalate force beyond what's needed for the mission,
responding to "insults" and stooping to vengeance. Others don't
understand mission at all. I heard a speech by a US Army general,
who began, "My job is to kill people." He could as easily and more
accurately have said, "My job is to protect Americans and that may
unfortunately involve killing people." That guy should be sacked
before he does any more damage.*

*There have been isolated human cultures that, like bono-
bos, shun war. When threatened, they have hired mercenaries or
allowed deviant insiders to fight on their behalf. The fighters were
exiled when the conflict ended — if the village survived — so as
not to contaminate the peaceful society. There are, in the modern*

world, far fewer isolated cultures. The characteristic, if not the peo-ple themselves, may die out.

So you're right that untrained pacifists may do more harm than good. Their attitude that violence never settles anything is naive. As Robert Heinlein noted, violence settled Hitler's hash pretty good. Work on yourself first, then work for peace! As an aikidoist, you are peaceable but skilled at forestalling conflict and applying minimum necessary violence. You position yourself in ways that communicate your strength and your intention, but you never "attack first." You don't interpose yourself between someone you want to protect and someone attacking her — except at the moment a blow is being struck — because it's unlikely that you understand what's really going on between them.

For the same reason, you would not assassinate even a despotic leader in cold blood. (Another hypothetical social experiment: Sup-pose all international conflicts were customarily settled by assassi-nation. Leaders would know before running for election that this is what would happen to them if they piss off another country. This would put a different complexion on politics, n'est ce pas?) You give everyone every opportunity to fix up their karma, until and unless they launch another attack. Only then is matching violence indi-cated — but if you are unprepared for their next attack, shame on you.

CONCLUSION: LOOKING FOR AIKIDO

◄o►

Much of aikido is physics and body mechanics. We know — or at least, scientists and doctors know — a lot about those things.

Yet aikido is also about attention and will. Attention and will are functions of consciousness. As the science press makes clear, and as this book has noted also, researchers have taken only baby steps toward understanding what consciousness is. Or where consciousness is.

And of course, O-Sensei said aikido is love.

This means a big fraction of what aikido is remains mysterious and invisible. It means "aikido techniques" are not aikido. Rather, the techniques are stepping stones that suggest a path toward aikido.

Traveling that path, you will find role models, teachers who make you think, I want to be like him or her. This is good if you internalize, and not just mimic, that teacher's manner and approach to aikido. Yet their personality is different from yours, and you will never exactly duplicate another person's aikido.

I think you already know what my parting advice is going to be: The only place to look for aikido is inside yourself. Practice sincerely, practice hard, and practice long. Aikido will reveal itself, emerging from your spirit and your practice.

Yet aikido is such a tease! It won't reveal everything at once. That would be impossible, as the well of aikido knowledge is bottomless. This is why aikido is a lifelong practice.

Glossary

—◄◦►—

Aiki taiso	Warm-up exercises that incorporate the basic movements that appear in aikido techniques.
Aikikai Honbu	The global aikido organization run by descendants of Ueshiba O-Sensei.
Aiki-ken	Sword work, as taught in aikido.
Atemi	A strike with the hand.
Bokken	A wooden practice sword.
Dera	A (Buddhist) temple.
Dogi, or *gi*	Martial arts practice uniform.
Dojo	Practice hall; place of training in the do (way).
Dojo-cho	Head of the dojo, usually the chief instructor.
Fune-kogi undo	"Boat-rowing" exercise in the aiki taiso.
Ganbatte kudasai	Please enjoy good luck!
Gokyo	Fifth teaching. An arm lock.
Hai	Japanese for "yes."
Hakama	Culotte worn by aikido practitioners, usually dark in color.
Happo giri	Eight-direction-cutting aiki taiso exercise.
Hara	The "one-point" in the lower abdomen.
Henka waza	Beginning a defense with one aikido technique, but completing it with a different technique. A change-up.

Honbu Dojo	Headquarter school of the global aikido organization run by descendants of Ueshiba O-Sensei.
Ikkyo	First teaching. Defense by rolling uke's elbow.
Iriminage	A class of throws using direct entry toward uke's body.
Jo	A wooden staff, between four and five feet long.
Jo nage	Throwing an uke who has attempted to grasp nage's jo.
Jo tori	Taking the jo from an uke who is attacking with it, subsequently throwing uke.
Kaeshi waza	A counter. Uke attacks, nage's defense is faulty, and uke becomes nage, performing a throw or takedown.
Kaisha	In Japan, a business corporation.
Kata	Shoulder. Or, a set-piece of movements, usually with weapon.
Kata-tori	Attack by grasping nage's shoulder.
Katate-tori	Attack by grasping nage's wrist.
Katori-ryu	A Japanese sword discipline, dating from the 1300s.
Ki	Inner energy that is summoned by an aikidoist's attention and will.
Kiai	Focusing energy in martial art and other demanding situations. Also, the well-known shout that, in martial art, accompanies the effort to focus.

Koan	A conundrum presented for the consideration of a Zen student. Possibly the most famous of koans is "What is the sound of one hand clapping?" To answer successfully, the student must embrace the seeming paradox, transcending the uncomfortably contradictory logic of the koan.
Kohai	A practitioner who is junior to you.
Kokyu	Breath. Sometimes used to mean 'timing,' and sometimes used as synonym for ki or ki-extension. When kokyu is the basis for a defense technique, the technique is called *kokyu nage*.
Kokyu dosa	Sometimes, *kokyu ho*. Exercise in which two persons sit knee to knee and try to off-balance each other. Not a test of strength, kokyu dosa requires making subtle connection with the opponent's center.
Kumitachi	Two-person set sword exercises.
Ma-ai	The customary and safe inter-personal distance from which we launch an attack-defense sequence with a partner.
Misogi	Ascetic training.
Nage	Person receiving an attack. Or, a throw.
Nikkyo	Second teaching, a momentarily painful control of uke's body via the wrist.
Sandan	A third-degree black belt.
Sankyo	Third teaching, a control of uke's body via the wrist.

Sayu nage	A.k.a. Sokumen iriminage. A reverse iriminage. At finish, nage contacts uke with nage's tricep area, rather than the bicep area.
Seiza	Sitting with legs folded under the body, usually with big toes crossing.
Sempai	A senior student, especially acting as mentor to a junior student. This is a relative term. If Gloria is a 1st dan, Joe is a 1st kyu, and Sam is a 2nd kyu, then Gloria may be sempai to Joe while Joe is sempai to Sam. In the movie *Rising Sun*, Wesley Snipes addressed Sean Connery (who played an older Japan scholar and a partner in investigation to Snipes' policeman character) as Sempai, while Connery called Snipes *Kohai*, meaning junior student.
Sen no sen	"Before the before." Extending one's attention to another, comprehending his or her posture, body type, range of motion, and state of attention, even before an attack develops. Attending to this principle helps predetermine the resolution of any ensuing attack, and prevents nage from reacting too late.
Sensei	Teacher. Literally, "before person," i.e., one who has gone before.
Shiho nage	The four-direction throw.

Shodan	A first-degree black belt. Aikido ranks start with 7th kyu (white belt) and work upward through 1st kyu (brown belt) and onward to shodan, black belt. In the black belt ranks, the numbering reverses itself, and higher dan ranks have higher numbers.
Shomen-uchi ikkyo undo	Aiki taiso in which one raises both arms and then cuts down, simulating raising and cutting with a sword.
Sokumen iriminage	See *Sayu nage*.
Suburi	Basic bokken and jo cuts and thrusts.
Tai sabaki	Body movement. Used to denote repositioning, especially nage's initial repositioning when receiving an attack.
Tenkan	Turning. One of the fundamental initial tai sabaki.
Tsutomete	Try hard!
Ude furi choyaku	An aiki-taiso involving swinging the arms (actually, simulating a sword-draw) while turning the body 180 degrees.
Uke	In Japanese martial art, person taking a fall. In aikido this is almost always the attacker.
Undo	Exercise.
Waza	Technique. In this book, the words technique and waza refer to any of aikido's named defenses, e.g., tenchi nage or kotae gaeshi.
Wing chun	A Chinese martial art.

Yokomen uchi	A strike to the side of the head.
Zanshin	Continuation of attention and consciousness.
Zengo undo	Tai sabaki that repeats the shomenu-chi-ikkyo exercise while turning body and attention 180 degrees.

About the Author

-<o>-

Fred Phillips, 6th Dan Aikikai, began his aikido training in early 1973. After breaking too many bones (his own, not other people's) during his year on the 1972 University of Texas judo team, Fred wandered into Bill Lee and Jay Portnow's aikido practice. (Bill and Jay were, respectively, students of Rod Kobayashi and Mitsunari Kanai.) After one class, Fred knew he would practice aikido the rest of his life.

When Fred won a graduate fellowship for research in Japan, he trained under Koichi Tohei Sensei at Ki Society HQ in Tokyo in 1975-76. In 1977, Kobayashi Sensei awarded Fred shodan, and recommended that he study with Fumio Toyoda Shihan in Chicago.

In the next decades, Fred ran dojos in Texas and Oregon under Toyoda Sensei's supervision. Shortly before he passed away in 2001, Toyoda Sensei advanced Fred to 5th Dan, re-aligned Aikido Association of America with World Aikikai Honbu, and registered his students' ranks with World Aikikai Honbu.

In 2004, Fred moved to Europe and enjoyed the hospitality of Aikido Tendo in Maastricht (the Netherlands). His European job took him to Peru, Malta, Cyprus, Belgium, Egypt, and Vietnam. In every country, he practiced with, or was invited to teach at, local aikido schools.

Between foreign postings, Fred lived in San Diego, California, training occasionally at the dojos of old friends Martin Katz and

Ken MacBeth and trying to learn Argentine tango at El Mundo del Tango.

From 2012 to 2015, Fred worked in Korea, training and teaching with the World Aikikai Honbu-affiliated Korean Aikido Federation. In 2015 he was appointed Distinguished Professor at Yuan Ze University in Taiwan, where he practiced and coached at Dong Wu Dojo (under Sūn Shìqiáng Sensei) and at the National Chengchi University and National Taiwan Normal University Aikido Clubs. Presently living in Albuquerque, USA, and practicing at Duke City Dojo, he continues to travel as guest and guest instructor at dojos worldwide. During the day he is a professor at University of New Mexico.

Fred's earlier book *The Conscious Manager: Zen for Decision Makers* reconciled many aikidoists' double lives — working in business or government during the day, and training in aikido at night.

For photos of Fred's aikido travels, see www.generalinformatics.com/CM/aikido.htm.

Fred was featured in Miles Kessler Sensei's book *50 Aikido Experts*. He occasionally posts material on Facebook, both on his own wall and on the group Aikido at the Leading Edge.